power plays

power plays

Overcome the Need for Control and Learn to Live with Strength and Integrity

Wayne Schmidt

wesleyan
publishing
house

Indianapolis, Indiana

Copyright © 2006 by Wesleyan Publishing House
Published by Wesleyan Publishing House
Indianapolis, Indiana 46250
Printed in the United States of America

ISBN-13: 978-0-89827-335-9
ISBN-10: 0-89827-335-8

Contents

Contents

Introduction

Margaret leaned back in her office chair, enjoying some quietness at the end of her workday. It had been a good day for her: she felt blessed to have a job she enjoyed and to work in an environment where she felt loved and respected. Margaret's financial services company was doing well, and she had the satisfaction of knowing that she was a contributor.

A senior project manager in the company's operations division, Margaret had spent the morning working on a couple of major projects and felt satisfied after completing a few more action steps on each of them. She'd had lunch with one of her direct reports, someone she had recently doubted would make it with the company. But Margaret had invested time in training this employee and was seeing signs of professional growth. That was an especially gratifying part of her job. Margaret had then spent most of the afternoon in a team meeting, where there was a lot of good pushback and peer accountability as the team grappled with the best way to achieve a critical goal. Afterward, she had caught up on e-mail and phone messages, and now sat reflecting on a day well spent. It was just past 5:00 p.m.

Margaret's thoughts shifted to home. While her work was satisfying, she had to admit that she was a bit apprehensive about what the dinner hour would bring. She and her husband were finding the parenting of teenagers to be challenging, and they weren't always on the same page with each other. Why, she wondered, was she so persuasive in her work yet unable to make progress in her relationships at home? She shuddered at the thought of the "cold war" taking place in her home. Margaret longed for the loving Christian family she'd heard described at church, but admitted that her goal was merely to negotiate a truce.

The thought of church reminded Margaret of the committee meeting scheduled for that evening. A few months ago, she had enthusiastically joined this committee, whose task was to update the church's strategic plan. The timing was right because a new pastor had recently arrived, bringing fresh energy to the somewhat complacent congregation. Because she functioned well on teams at work, Margaret thought it would be a natural place for her to jump in and make a contribution.

But for some reason, the committee had bogged down. While the pastor was brimming with ideas, he didn't seem to adjust well to the culture of the church and community. Some of the committee members—even those who had been involved in the search process that brought the new pastor to town—seemed resistant to owning up to the challenges their church faced and empowering the pastor to make necessary changes. Margaret began to wonder if this church committee would turn out like some others she had experienced—lots of meetings but little momentum.

As Margaret reflected on the evening ahead, it dawned on her that the most important places in her life—work, home, church—were interwoven. She generally tried to compartmentalize her life, focusing most of her energy on whichever environment she happened to be in. Yet now they all ran together in her thinking. Her experience, good or bad, in one area invariably spilled over to another. Margaret cared deeply about each of the areas in her life. Why, she wondered, did she lack the power to make a difference in each place?

The clocked showed 5:29 p.m. as Margaret cleared her desk and threw a couple of strategic planning books into her briefcase—perhaps they would be helpful in tonight's meeting. As she reached to shut down her computer, a popup message appeared on the screen. "Make dinner: 30 minutes overdue." She sighed, remembering that it was her turn to prepare the evening meal. "Time for round two," she said to herself and headed out the door.

Power Plays

Power. From the beginning of human history, God has chosen to entrust it to people. Power is a fact of life, and we all exercise it in some measure. What is power? It's the capacity to turn intention into action. Without power, intentions are nothing more than wishful thinking. With power, intentions can move from day dreaming to life changing. Margaret exercised power—or attempted to—in each of the three areas of her life. At work, she turned her intention into action by successfully managing the work of a group of employees. Things happened because Margaret willed them to happen and took the appropriate actions to make them reality. At home and at church, Margaret was frustrated by her lack of power. She felt powerless to improve her family relationships and to effect change in her congregation. In all cases, she was attempting to exercise power.

How do we exercise power? Dr. Richard Swenson says that "power is made up of factors such as skills, time, emotional strength, physical strength, spiritual vitality, finances, social supports and education."[1] I would further distill these factors to identify four basic ingredients of a Christian's *power capacity*—that is, the believer's potential to exercise power. They are

- Inspiration
- Intelligence
- Influence
- Investment

Inspiration

For a follower of Christ, inspiration is more than positive thinking or self-motivation. We understand that which is inspired to be *God-breathed*. So to be inspired is to know that God's Spirit has "breathed" something into your spirit. This ingredient of power capacity is foundational for the Christian, for we must know whether it is God's Spirit that is prompting our intentions and empowering our actions. If it is not, then our capacity for power is self-generated and likely self-serving. This ingredient of power is fundamentally spiritual.

Intelligence

By intelligence, I'm not referring to the I.Q. of an individual, though that may be an element of this ingredient of power. This term refers to intelligence gathering, an activity that every government and most businesses spend a good deal of money on, but which most people do in less formal (and less expensive) ways. This ingredient of power capacity asks the question "Do I know what I need to know?" This intelligence includes information, expertise, and the accurate assessment of people and cultures. This ingredient of the capacity for power is fundamentally mental.

Influence

Influence is the ability to relate effectively to others. We often think of relating to others as a function of personality—being extroverted or introverted, choleric or sanguine. Personality may be a factor in determining influence; but when it comes to the capacity for power, influence includes a person's networks, endorsements by others, approval, and legitimacy in his or her sphere of influence. This ingredient of power asks the question "How well do I relate to others?" and is fundamentally social.

Investment

Investment concerns a person's will and position. By *will,* I mean the courage to act and the willingness to commit necessary resources. By *position*, I mean the potential to carry out an action, part of which may at times be beyond my direct control. Investment asks the question "Do I have both the will and the resources to turn this intention into action?" This ingredient of the capacity for power is both volitional and positional.

So the capacity for power involves four ingredients, which involve the critical life areas of spirit, mind, relationships, will, and position. This means that our power capacity—our ability to turn intention to action at any given point—is an index of our spiritual health, intellectual acumen, relational integrity, and our willingness and ability to commit the time, energy, finances, and other resources that may be necessary. While we, like Margaret, may feel powerless at times, we do have the capacity for power in nearly every area of our lives.

The Stewardship of Power

As Christians, we are commissioned to use power, and we are responsible to use it in godly ways. We are stewards of power. A steward is someone who manages something that belongs to another. God entrusts His power to us, and we're accountable for the way in which we use it. Just as we're to be good stewards of our time, money and abilities, we're to be good stewards of power.

Proper stewardship of power involves all ingredients of one's capacity for power, used in harmony. Think of these ingredients as a musical chord—a power chord, if you will.

Good stewardship of power orchestrates inspiration, ideas, influence, and investment to bring about a result that both glorifies God and edifies others. Poor stewardship of power—that is, the abuse of power—is self-generated and self-serving.

As with any other area of stewardship, the capacity to exercise power presents an opportunity for either wise use or abuse. Sadly, the use and abuse of power is rarely discussed among Christians. To overlook a theme so central in Scripture is not simply unfortunate; it is also detrimental to the coming of God's kingdom into our lives, homes, workplaces, and churches.

God's first communication with the human race involved the stewardship of power. "God blessed them and said to them, 'Be fruitful and increase in number; fill the earth and *subdue* it. *Rule* over the fish of the sea and the birds of the air and over every living creature that moves on the ground" (Gen. 1:28, emphasis mine). To *subdue* and to *rule* are manifestations of power. Therefore, human beings have a mandate from God to exercise power on His behalf. What is more, God created man and woman with the *capacity* to rule and subdue—to exercise power.

Not surprisingly, the first temptation involved the use of power. In Genesis 3, Satan challenges God's authority and tempts human beings with pride and power. "For God knows that when you eat of it your eyes will be opened, and you will *be like God*, knowing good and evil" (Gen. 3:5, emphasis mine). Adam and Eve succumbed to that temptation, attempting to seize greater power for themselves. It was the original power grab, and ever since then people have been trading the blessed life that results from submitting to God and stewarding His power for the mirage of omnipotence that comes from exercising power as if it originated with them.

Embezzlement of Power

The opposite of stewardship is embezzlement. Malachi 3:8–9 makes that clear concerning the management of money: "'Will a man rob God?' Yet you rob me. But you ask, 'How do we rob you?' In tithes and offerings. You are under a curse—the whole nation of you—because you are robbing me."

How do we rob God? Through embezzlement: by taking something that belongs to God, something He has entrusted to us for His purposes and using it instead for our own ends. It is a common enough temptation. Consider the situation of an employee who manages money for a business owner. After a while the employee may begin to feel a sense of entitlement about the money that passes through his hands every day. In time, he may begin to use the money to benefit himself in ways the owner never intended. He embezzles. Malachi points out that we do the same thing by appropriating money that is rightfully God's for our own use.

Just as we may embezzle money, we may embezzle power. We may forget that the power we exercise in our homes, our churches, our workplaces—indeed, in our own lives—is God's power and that we are simply managers of it. We can begin to use that power for our own purposes rather than to fulfill the will of God, who entrusted it to us.

Power Plays

I've seen people blossom in environments where power is used with humility and integrity. In these environments people are empowered by God and by others to live out their divine purpose. Sadly, I've also seen people wither, even cower, when power is abused. In its wake, the abuse of power leaves distorted images of God and broken relationships with others.

Misuse of Power

Power plays in the church, especially negative ones, are some-times obvious. I'm not speaking of physical wrestling matches, though I nearly witnessed one as a child! In the church where I grew up, there was a clock placed prominently on the front wall of the sanctuary, just to the left of the platform. Everyone sitting in the con-gregation could plainly see what time it was, how long the pastor had preached, and when the service was about to go into "overtime."

Our pastor must have decided that the clock was getting too much attention. I don't remember if he announced his intention or simply carried it out, but one Sunday when we arrived for church, the hands were missing from the clock. The clock couldn't be removed entirely because it was built into the wall; but with the hands removed, the clock watchers had lost their prized possession.

After the service, I saw a man in the narthex yelling at the pastor and coming very near to physically assaulting him. I'd never seen a pastor spoken to in that way, let alone threatened with violence. I knew the man who was cornering the pastor. I fact, I viewed him as being one of the "saints" in the church—at least I had before that day.

When we got home, my parents debriefed me on the situation. The man's family had donated the clock that was so prominently displayed in the church. He was deeply offended that the pastor had disabled this symbol of the family's generosity. His anger got the best of him, and he wasn't going to be satisfied until the pastor replaced the hands on the clock. As I remember, the hands were back on the clock the next Sunday!

Our pastor, because of his position of leadership in the church, felt he had the power to remove the clock hands. The church member, because of his financial contribution to the church, felt that he had the power to prevent it. Some might conclude that because the hands were returned to the clock, the church member was more powerful. Yet his inappropriate approach to the pastor may have reduced that man's capacity for power by undermining his credibility with others. The man's investment was very high, but his influence suffered greatly as a result of the encounter.

Disuse of Power

Most power struggles are not so visible—or physical—as the one involving the church clock. In fact, many power plays draw their energy from subtlety. And very often, power plays aren't isolated to one arena of life. Power plays at work can spill over into the home. Power plays in marriage can spill over into parenting. Power plays in the home can spill over into the church.

One of the most painful realities I've had to confront as a pastor is the abuse of children. It breaks a pastor's heart to discover that family members who profess faith in Christ have verbally, physically, or sexually abused children. Early in my ministry I was ill-prepared to face one such event, and it nearly split our church.

In its beginning stages, the church that I led was a small, close-knit group. In many ways, we were the "one big happy family" that many long for the church to be. I knew practically everyone, and the majority of the people knew each other as well. Like most congregations, our church family had several extended family groups within it.

An uncle in one of those extended family groups was accused of sexually abusing his niece while babysitting her in his home. The girl's parents, who were the man's brother and sister-in-law, also members of the church, appropriately reported this to the authorities. An investigation ensued. Although the man consistently maintained his innocence, he was found guilty. If indeed guilty, this uncle's use of power in molesting his niece was abuse of power at its very worst. The extended family was split in its opinion about the matter. Some stood with the sister who was married to the man accused of abuse. Others steadfastly surrounded the sister whose child was reportedly abused.

As a pastor, I naïvely took the stance that because the alleged incident had taken place within a private home and within a family, and because the authorities were involved and were ultimately responsible for deciding the case, it was unnecessary for the leadership of our church to process the issue and determine a response to both sides. Inevitably, as church people began to hear of the situation from one side or the other, they took sides. Eventually, the church's leaders chose sides. I maintained the untenable position of neutrality, believing that the church was somehow above the fray and that discussing the issue as a board was an unnecessary invasion of family privacy.

I now know that the abuse of power within a family often spills over into a church. The sense of righteous indignation one side felt about the abuse quickly became righteous indignation toward the inaction of the church. Others argued that even if the uncle were guilty, he was experiencing the legal consequences of his action and, therefore, was all the more in need of our grace and forgiveness.

People began to leave the church. Some board members chose to resign, and others elected to not serve again when their terms expired. Some who had been supportive of me as a pastor considered my inaction to be something more than an error in judgment; they were convinced it was enough to disqualify me from spiritual leadership. I had the capacity to make a difference, and I failed to be a good steward of the power entrusted to me. Observing this power vacuum, others stepped in and used their own power in a variety of ways—some appropriate and others abusive.

The Integration of Power

Power plays cannot be compartmentalized. What happens at work will affect the family. What happens in the family can involve church. What happens in church can create tension in a marriage. Throughout this book we will explore five *arenas of power* and discover the ways that power is used in each.

We will begin, appropriately, by learning about God's power to transform the self in the spiritual and eternal realm. We will then look at the very practical ways power can be wisely used in marriage, in the family, in the workplace, and in the church. We'll devote a little extra time to examining power plays in church because many people prefer to remain in denial about the effects of power and the destruction it can cause in local churches. Along the way, we'll apply a number of biblical principles and practical insights on the stewardship of power. We will discover—

- How Jesus dealt with religious power brokers
- The spiritual dimensions of power
- The "power tools" used in building a marriage
- The different power styles used by different people
- How parental power changes as children develop
- How wielding power at work can change a person
- Why power-full pastors or lay leaders can make or break a church
- How power-blocks can keep a church from carrying out its mission

We will also see three types of power users in action: power brokers, power grabbers, and power shifters. We'll hear their stories of real-life power plays. We will hear of a man who "powered up" on his wife and destroyed their storybook marriage. We'll learn from a man who discovered the value of sitting lightly in the *power seat* at work. And we will encounter a pastor whose run-in with a powerful church boss ended his ministry at that church. We will see in these stories the damaging effects of the inappropriate use of power, but we'll also see the tremendous positive impact that can be made by the proper stewardship of power.

Power plays can have both positive and negative effects. Power functions in people's lives and relationships in a variety of ways, so the challenge is to harness power for positive purposes while recognizing that it can be abused when we attempt to reach beyond our authority or ability.

But this book is not about *other* people. It is about you. Through this book you will learn about your own use of power. You will discover the capacity for power that you possess, and you will see how you have both used power and been impacted by its use. And as you apply these principles to your life, you will overcome the tendency that we all have to abuse our power in order to control others and will instead be motivated to live with strength and integrity. As your stewardship of power improves, you will see positive changes in your home, family, workplace, church—and, ultimately, in yourself.

To begin, make an assessment of your power style. What power do you have, and how do you use it?

The Power to Be

Arena of Power:	Self
Source of Power:	The Holy Spirit
Power Principle:	I have the God-given capacity to turn vision into reality.

Ken was confused. It had been a little over a year since he, a thirty-four-year-old automotive engineer, had made a commitment to Jesus Christ and received assurance of his salvation. That profession of faith had not been an act of desperation but had followed a long process of inquiry: Ken was grateful to have a strong marriage and good relationships with his children. His work was challenging and, for the most part, fulfilling. Yet Ken had become restless, plagued by a nagging sense that there was something more to life. Deep down, he felt empty. Though not a religious person, he began to wonder if the lasting significance he longed for might be found in religion.

In keeping with his analytical style, Ken began to research various world religions. His research led him to the conclusion that he could become an adherent to only one of them. While he'd heard others say that they believe all the world's religions are right and that all ways lead to God, Ken's study revealed a basic incompatibility between the core beliefs of each religion. What one religion taught about salvation ruled out what the others held. If one of them were true, intellectual integrity demanded the rest be false.

Further research led Ken to the conclusion that Christianity was the religion most likely to be true. He began to study the Bible and became increasingly convinced that Jesus was the way to salvation. During the course of his search, Ken checked out several local churches and eventually connected with one where he also became engaged in a small group. This small group was filled with sincere believers. After awhile, and with their encouragement, Ken placed his faith in Jesus Christ as Savior.

One of the things that had most attracted Ken to Christianity was its promise that life could truly be different than it was. He was intrigued with statements in Scripture like "If anyone is in Christ, he is a new creation; the old has gone, the new has come!" (2 Cor. 5:17). Ken was filled with hope as he read these words from 1 Thessalonians 5:23–24: "May God himself, the God of peace, sanctify you through and through. May your whole spirit, soul and body be kept blameless at the coming of our Lord Jesus Christ. The one who calls you is faithful and he will do it." These weren't simply pious platitudes to Ken—they were expressions of an experience that a Christian could pray for and expect to happen. He saw further evidence of this as he read in the book of Acts and saw that the lives of early Christians were truly transformed by God's Spirit and that their faith was contagious to those around them.

Yet here was the problem: as a new Christian, Ken was receiving mixed messages from other believers about whether God's power was still operative today. Some sincere Christians humbly acknowledged an inability to overcome what they described as their "sinful nature." Ken listened to their prayers, in which they offered confessions such as "Forgive the many sins in word, thought, and deed that I've committed today." These believers often referred to their faith as a private matter, not to be spoken of with others because it was between them and God. While they hoped others would see the difference in their lives and be attracted to the gospel, Ken wondered, "What difference?"

On the other hand, Ken also observed some equally sincere Christ-followers who were convinced there was no ingrained sin within them that God couldn't root out. They would often pray for purity of heart and love for others. These believers were quick to offer the disclaimer that they were far from perfect and had a lot of room for spiritual growth, yet they seemed to believe that God could change their lives—and actually would. It was obvious that they expected God to give them victory inside and out. As a result, they seemed to possess a holy optimism. They believed that God's grace not only provided forgiveness but also empowered transformation. They seemed eager to talk with others about the difference God was making in their lives.

23

"So," Ken wondered, "What can I really expect from God? Will He change me—deep down? Will He enable me to make a difference in the lives of others?"

If power is the capacity to turn intention into action, then Ken's questions are really questions about power—God's power in the world and in our lives. Without power, Ken realized, his intentions would be nothing more than wishful thinking. So what he, and the rest of us, is really asking is this: Is the power of God available to me?

While we may at times feel impotent, all of us are power-full people because we have been empowered by God. He gives us the basic human abilities to think and to act, to turn our intentions into action. However, some have rightly observed that the human will is limited, at best. As Paul compellingly illustrates in Romans 7, we are the most miserable of creatures when we will to behave one way yet constantly fail to act on those intentions. Our wills are weak.

Yet God's will is powerful. As Paul goes on to describe in Romans 8, God's Holy Spirit empowers us to act. By His grace, we are able to live different lives than before. By God's grace, we are transformed. When we respond to God through faith, *He* empowers us to be something that we were not. So, by the power of God's Spirit, we can hope to realize genuine life change. Let's explore the issue of God's power to change the self from three angles:

- Inspiration   God's power *to* me
- Transformation   God's power *in* me
- Expression   God's power *through* me

Inspiration: God's Power *to* Me

As we begin this discussion, let's first acknowledge a basic attribute of God: *omnipotence*. This term, which combines the words *omni* and *potent,* expresses the reality that God is all-powerful. He has the capacity to turn all of His intentions into actions. That idea is captured by the words of a banner that I once saw displayed at the front of a church: "God Can." Anything that God wills to do, He can do. We must acknowledge that fact.

Yet we must also recognize that God sovereignly chooses to reserve some of His power just for himself. So while God shares some of His power with His children, we are not omnipotent. The power He shares with us still belongs to Him, and we are managers of the portion He entrusts to us.

God's Power to Us

The Bible uses several words to describe God's power. Three of them are particularly helpful in understanding how God's power relates to us.

Authority. The first term is *authority* (from the Greek word *exousia*), which refers to freedom of action. This is the right to act, the right to exercise power. God has authority in that He enjoys both the freedom and the right to exercise power as He chooses. God's authority is absolute and unrestricted. His power is His own, and He has the authority to use it. Jesus, speaking to His disciples, said "All authority in heaven and on earth has been given to me" (Matt. 28:18). Later He said to them, "It is not for you to know the times or dates the Father has set by his own authority" (Acts 1:7). Jesus made clear that

25

God's authority is unlimited and that He chooses to reserve some of it for himself.

When the term *authority* is used in relation to human beings, it designates authority that is delegated by God. For example, God grants some of His authority to government officials: "Everyone must submit himself to the governing authorities, for there is no authority except that which God has established" (Rom. 13:1). God also delegated authority to the apostles, as Paul writes, "For even if I boast somewhat freely about the authority the Lord gave us for building you up rather than pulling you down, I will not be ashamed of it" (2 Cor. 10:8). So God chooses to entrust the freedom and right to exercise power to people whom He selects. God grants authority to us in some measure.

Ability. A second term used to describe God's power is *ability* (from the Greek word *dunamis*), which refers to the capacity to act. From the Greek root of this word, we derive such words as *dynamo, dynamic,* and *dynamite.* The Greek word *dunamis* is used over one hundred times in the New Testament, often applied to believers. Jesus wanted His early disciples to know that this God-given ability was entrusted to them. He said, "But you will receive power when the Holy Spirit comes on you; and you will be my witnesses in Jerusalem, and in all Judea and Samaria, and to the ends of the earth" (Acts 1:8). The disciples would receive God's power; they would be enabled to act. Yet that power was given for God's purpose—so that they would be His witnesses.

Activity. A final word in our sampler of power terms is *activity* (from the Greek word *energema*). This is applied power—power in action. From the Greek root of this word comes our word *energy*. The Bible describes God's Word as active: "For the Word of God is living and active" (Heb. 4:12). The term is also used to describe effective ministry. Paul wrote, "But I will stay on at Ephesus until Pentecost, because a great door for effective work has opened to me, and there are many who oppose me" (1 Cor. 16:8–9). As believers, we have God's power in that we exercise it; we act effectively in His name.

So taken together, these terms taken from Scripture tell us that God has the freedom and right to exercise His power, that He is able to do so, and, as a matter of fact, He does do so. We also know that on occasion God entrusts these dimensions of His power to us, which He has been doing since the dawn of creation (see Gen. 1:26–28).

Qualifying to Receive God's Power

According to Scripture, it is fully appropriate for Christians to be power-full. God intends to share His power with us, and He intends for us to use it. Personally, I want to receive all of the power that God wishes to share with me. Yet there is something inherently dangerous about power and its impact on a person. Like dynamite, it must be handled with care. And not everyone is entrusted by God with power. There are three questions that must be answered if we are to be candidates to receive God's power.

Question one: Am I sure that the power I'm experiencing has its source in God? The Bible makes it clear that there are various spiritual power sources that impact people. One way to conceptualize these

27

forces is as a vertical continuum with God's Spirit on one pole, evil spirits on the opposite pole, and the human spirit somewhere in the middle.

God's Spirit

Human spirit

Evil spirits

Power can be evil. Increasingly, the culture around us either denies the reality of evil spirits or reduces Satan to a poltergeist or cartoon character. Yet the Bible clearly states that forces of evil do exist. In Ephesians 6:10–12, Paul instructs Christians on the basics of spiritual battle:

> Finally, be strong in the Lord and in his mighty power. Put on the full armor of God so that you can take your stand against the devil's schemes. For our struggle is not against flesh and blood, but against the rulers, against the authorities, against the powers of this dark world and against the spiritual forces of evil in the heavenly realms.

There is a dark side to the world, and it is not a figment of some filmmaker's imagination. In the Western world, we often underestimate the impact of power plays in the spiritual realm. In some other cultures, power encounters between the forces of good and evil are much more evident. While completing doctoral training, I interacted with a professor who had spent many years on the mission field. He showed me the videotape of a baptism service he'd conducted in a country where oppression by evil spirits was regularly evidenced. As a girl was about to be baptized, a voice that could only be described as unnatural and evil came out of her. She thrashed on the ground as the missionary called upon the evil spirit to leave her. The evil spirit responded audibly to the missionary's commands given in the name of Jesus, and finally exited with great reluctance. Frankly, even given this professor's great credibility, if I hadn't seen it, I'm not sure I would have believed it.

Is Satan less at work in Western cultures? Hardly. He is a wolf in sheep's clothing and is only rendered more powerful by the fact that his work here is more subtle. You and I may not hear audible voices and see visible evidence of Satan's presence, but the power struggle between good and evil is just as real here as in other parts of the world. We, as Christians, are to be aware of Satan's schemes and strength. We are to draw our confidence to be strong and stand firm from God's mighty power. The Bible assures us that the powers opposing God will ultimately be defeated. The power of the wicked is temporary.

In the middle of the continuum, I've placed the human spirit. Human power has its roots in the reality that all humans are creations of God and are made in His image. Inherent within us is a certain level of delegated power. We recognize this power when we speak of an individual who possesses a "powerful personality." Even in the lives of people who express no allegiance to Christ, we notice the "power of positive thinking" at work. As people develop their own skills and influence, they become more powerful. All of us have a certain capacity to turn intention into action. We all have some power.

Because of the way in which human beings are created, it is possible for the human spirit to draw power from the potential within itself.

Many secular scholars have given themselves to the study of human potential. This power is limited, however. We are created in the image of God, but we are not gods. We are not omnipotent.

As its placement in the middle of the continuum indicates, the human spirit can also draw power from either end of the scale. Human beings can gain access to power that comes from within themselves—or from external sources that are evil, or from God. On the right end of the continuum is the power that resides in God's Spirit. This power is available to believers also, and it is the power that was described in our sampler of biblical power terms. God's power is above all other powers.

So the first consideration for those of us wishing to exercise power in our lives is to determine the source of that power. Is it power that comes from within us? If so, what are its limits? If the source of power comes from beyond us, is that power from God? Does it match the description of God's power from Scripture? Does it come from His authority? Do we intend to use it for His purpose? Are there signs that our attempted use of power is either self-generated or self-serving? Or, worse yet, motivated by evil?

Question two: How do I disqualify myself from receiving God's power? The second question for those seeking to receive God's power can be answered with a single word: pride. "God opposes the proud, but gives grace to the humble" (1 Pet. 5:5). It is paradoxical that many of the people who are the most humble are entrusted by God with the use of great power; however, the more they experience a power surge from God in their lives, the greater will be their temptation to take pride in what God has given them or what has been accomplished through it. Some even begin to think of this power as their own. Then, as they become proud of "their" power, God removes His power from their lives and begins to oppose them.

When I moved to the community of Kentwood, Michigan, to plant the church where I now serve, I arranged interviews with various community leaders. This was a good way both to introduce myself to them and to see the community through their eyes. I met with the superintendent of schools, the police chief, and the mayor. While having lunch with the mayor, I discovered that he was a believer and a man of great wisdom. Although that appointment occurred more that two decades ago, I still remember a bit of advice he gave me that day. He said, "Wayne, power has a tendency to corrupt. Not only political or economic power, but even *spiritual* power has caused many to stumble." Over the years I've seen the truth of this warning played out over and over again. When God gives people power for His purposes, pride may deceive them into thinking that *they* are the source of that power and that it exists for them to use as they wish.

In the Old Testament we read the story of a great king of Judah named Uzziah. He was only sixteen years old when he became king, and he reigned for fifty-two years. We're told of Uzziah's success as a leader, of the wars he won and the building projects he completed. But as he experienced more of God's blessing and was entrusted with more of God's power, a change occurred. "His fame spread far and wide, for he was greatly helped until he became powerful. But after Uzziah became powerful, his pride led to his downfall. He was unfaithful to the L ORD his God" (2 Chron. 26:15–16). Power led Uzziah to become prideful, and that pride invited God's opposition.

There's a story of another great king in the Old Testament. This king ruled the most powerful kingdom of the world. He conquered the nation of Israel along with many other nations. The prophet Daniel tells us of this great king, Nebuchadnezzar, and his incredible kingdom. This king's power also led him to pride:

He said, "Is not this the great Babylon I have built as the royal residence, by my mighty power and for the glory of my majesty?"

The words were still on his lips when a voice came from heaven, "This is what is decreed for you, King Nebuchadnezzar: Your royal authority has been taken from you. You will be driven away from people and will live with the wild animals; you will eat grass like cattle. Seven times will pass by for you until you acknowledge that the Most High is sovereign over the kingdoms of men and gives them to anyone he wishes" (Dan. 4:30–32). When the king became proud, God sent him out to graze in the fields until he understood Who was really powerful and who was not. I regularly remind myself—any time I try a power grab with God in an attempt to get my hands on His power and glory—that He can just as easily send me out to graze in the fields!

Ultimately, Nebuchadnezzar learned his lesson. After grazing for awhile, he lifted his eyes toward heaven and praised God by saying,

His dominion is an eternal dominion; his kingdom endures from generation to generation. All the peoples of the earth are regarded as nothing. He does as he pleases, with the powers of heaven and the peoples of the earth. No one can hold back his hand or say to him: "What have you done?" (Dan. 4:34–35).

Many people engage in power plays with God. They enter a battle of wills with Him or utilize sophisticated spiritual defense tactics. But in the end, God's power prevails.

When Jesus was about to begin His public ministry, the Holy Spirit led Him into the desert to be tempted (see Matt. 4:1–11). There are many ways to characterize these temptations, but I'm convinced that one element of the temptation of Christ involved His use of power. Satan tempted Jesus to use the power His Father had entrusted to Him for His own purposes. Jesus had to settle that power play before He began His public ministry—and He did. He clearly affirmed that God's power was to be used for God's purpose alone.

Those of us who aspire to exercise power—even the power to effect change within ourselves—must resolve a similar power play. We must settle the question of pride. What is the source of your power? And what is its purpose? Has your attitude toward power changed over time?

Question three: How do I develop my capacity to receive God's power? As a Christian, I want to grow in my capacity for power— that is, in my ability to operate under God's authority and in His power. I desire to exercise spiritual authority as I relate to my family, fulfill my employment responsibilities, and carry out my ministry. As I look back over my life, I recognize that God has utilized a variety of means to help me improve my stewardship of His power.

Sometimes the greatest insights in life come from the greatest disappointments. These negative experiences can come when others abuse their power over us or when we ourselves fail to submit to God-given authorities. These negative power plays create dissonance in our lives as we are unsettled by what we see. As a result, we grow.

As a twenty-one-year-old college graduate, I felt that God had placed in me the strong desire to plant a church. In my youthful over-confidence, I saw myself as the leader of this venture, and was initially disappointed when I was informed that I would be appointed as the assistant pastor in the church to be formed. The senior pastor was to be Dick Wynn, who was serving full time with Youth for Christ. He would serve the church part time in order to provide overall leadership.

Early on I asked Dick questions such as "How long do you see yourself serving the church?" and "As other staff members are added, will they report to you or to me?" Deep down, I wanted to become the one with more power as the church developed. But as time passed, I realized how unprepared I was to give leadership to this church and how much I benefited being mentored by a more mature leader. What I initially resisted became a great blessing, submitting to the authority structure God had put in place for our church. A couple of years later when Dick announced that he was being promoted within the Youth for Christ organization and would be leaving the area, I found myself hesitant to step into the role of senior pastor. Over those two years, I had learned how much I needed to be under authority, and I had realized the great responsibility that accompanies the privilege of exercising authority.

When we see power misused or abused, it often prompts us to search for examples of the legitimate usage of power. By observing those who utilize power with humility, we can gain an even greater understanding of the proper stewardship of power. Dick Wynn set that example for me. Another mentor, Dr. Russ Mawby, former CEO of the Kellogg Foundation, showed me how to serve behind the scenes in order to make good things happen and to allow other people to get the credit for it. Russ delighted in being a catalyst for great endeavors that would impact his city, even though people had no idea that he was involved in any way.

When we see the use of power modeled well by others, we have a growing desire to model legitimate authority ourselves. And we experience the blessing of utilizing power to serve others, which Jesus identified as a characteristic of greatness (Matt. 23:11–12). The deeper level of satisfaction that comes from exercising humility surpasses the temporary high that comes from displaying pride. When we exercise proper stewardship of power, we find that it leads to deeper relationships at home, at work, and at church.

Choosing proper role models for the stewardship of power is invaluable for developing your own capacity for power. What examples of both the use and abuse of power have you witnessed? What lessons can be drawn from each? What does your reaction to these instances of the stewardship of power reveal about your own motivations?

Preparing for the Opportunity to Steward Power

The more we consistently exercise authority in appropriate ways, the more we gain new opportunities. In the words of the master in Jesus' parable of the talents, "You have been faithful with a few things; I will put you in charge of many things" (Matt. 25:21, 23).

In his book *The Making of a Leader*, Robert Clinton identifies this typical progression in the development of a leader:

1. Negative lessons in authority.
2. A search for and understanding of legitimate authority.
3. Desire to model legitimate authority.
4. Insights about spiritual authority.
5. Increasing use of spiritual authority as a source of power.[1]

Many of the lessons I've learned about the stewardship of power have been the result of conflict. I'm amazed at the number of times I've experienced conflict at home, at work, or in ministry only to discover that there was some power play at the root of it. In my early years of ministry, as I struggled more routinely with authority issues, I was impacted by the writings of Watchman Nee. Summarizing many of Nee's principles, Clinton identifies what he calls the Ten Commandments of Spiritual Authority:

1. One who learns spiritual authority as the power base of ministry must recognize the essential Source of all authority—God.
2. God's delegated authority does not belong to the person exercising it—that person is just a channel.

3. The channel of delegated authority is responsible to God for how that authority is exercised.

4. A leader is one who recognizes God's authority manifested in real-life situations.

5. Subjection to authority means that a person is subject to God himself and not to the channel through which that authority comes.

6. Rebellion against authority means that a person is not subjecting himself to God, though it may appear that the person is rejecting some impure manifestation of God's authority through a human channel.

7. People who are under God's authority look for and recognize spiritual authority and willingly place themselves under it.

8. Spiritual authority is never exercised for one's own benefit, but for those under it.

9. A person in spiritual authority does not have to insist on obedience—that is the moral responsibility of the follower.

10. God is responsible to defend spiritual authority.[2]

I've found it helpful to reflect on my life in light of each of these principles. For instance, when I read the tenth commandment, I must consider the degree to which I am willing to trust God in situations where others doubt my wisdom or leadership. I realize how defensive I tend to be when probing questions are asked or people push back on my viewpoints. To become a steward of God's power is to be granted a trust. And anyone who is given a trust will be held accountable for it. If we are to become stewards of God's power, we must examine ourselves so that we are prepared for the responsibility that will attend such an opportunity.

Transformation: God's Power *in* Me

I'm an optimist. That isn't because I'm convinced that people are inherently good or have unlimited capabilities. I'm not. I am an optimist because I am convinced that the power of God's Spirit is available to every believer that seeks Him. Our future can be different from our past. Sinful patterns in our lives can be broken. As God's love and grace transform us, we can love others deeply and purely. By the power of God's Spirit, this transformation can engulf individuals, families, workplaces, churches, communities, and even nations.

Not all believers are optimists, however. The more pessimistic among us focus on the devastating realities of sin and the failure of so many Christians to live differently from the world around them. As some Christians see it, we'll be transformed when we get to heaven, but on earth we're left to struggle along in sin. They view this struggle not only as an outward battle but also as an inner one, believing that Christians must live in conflict with their sinful natures as long as this life lasts.

While I deeply respect the many sincere believers who hold that view, I am convinced that the power of God—and not the reality of sin—should be our focus. If we do not believe something is possible, we probably won't seek it. And the release of God's transforming power in our lives takes place when God graciously gives us the ability to surrender ourselves completely to Him. Transformation begins with consecration.

The Process of Transformation

The process by which our lives our transformed by the power of God is outlined in Romans 12:1–2. That process begins with our willingness to make ourselves completely available to God. Paul writes, "Therefore, I urge you brothers, in view of God's mercy, to offer your bodies as living sacrifices, holy and pleasing to God—this is your spiritual act of worship" (Rom. 12:1). That is *consecration*—the offering of ourselves to God as living sacrifices.

This act of consecration opens the door for transformation. Paul continues, "Do not conform any longer to the pattern of this world, but be transformed by the renewing of your mind. Then you will be able to test and approve what God's will is—his good, pleasing and perfect will" (Rom. 12:2). It is an act of our will, prompted and empowered by God's Spirit, that brings us to consecrate ourselves. It is an act of God's Spirit that transforms the lives we present to Him.

Some have mistakenly focused only on the human side of this equation. They see the change in their lives as a result of their willingness to submit to Jesus Christ as their Lord. While this surrender is a crucial prerequisite to transformation, that human act—or rather, that human response to God's prompting—does not make us any different than we were before. Rather, that act of submission is a holy invitation for God's Spirit to completely fill our lives and to break the power of sinful patterns in our lives. It is God who has the power to transform us. Our role in the process is to allow that transformation by surrendering our will to God's. In my personal daily devotions, I occasionally utilize devotional literature in addition to prayer, Bible reading, and journaling. One resource I've returned to on several occasions is *Praying in the Wesleyan Spirit,* in which author Paul Chilcote renders some of the classic sermons of John Wesley as prayers. Reading these prayers has elevated my faith in the power of God's Spirit to transform a human life. Chilcote writes,

God of Perfect Love,

You call me to be perfect even as you are perfect. That is a monumental claim upon my life. Despite the fact that this call to be completely conformed to the image of Christ—to be absolutely Christlike in my life—is offensive to many, I will strive to open my life to the transforming power of your perfecting love. My prayer is that I might become daily more and more like Jesus, your Son.

The perfection to which you call me certainly does not mean that I will ever be free from ignorance or mistakes or infirmities or temptation; neither is it a call to absolute perfection, for only your unconditional love is perfect in this sense.

Rather you call me quite simply to develop such a close and loving relationship with you that I would never want to do anything to separate myself from that love or withhold it from anyone else. You call me to be loving as Christ was loving, in every relationship and at all times. And if I live by your grace in this way, then I will always be able to look you in the face without fear and with love in my eyes.[3]

It is God's will that I be holy and loving. That is God's intention, and He has the power— the capacity to translate this intention into action. The pathway to God's transforming power requires my humility and surrender. I'm discovering that, more often than not, it also involves brokenness. In the words of Larry Crabb,

> Brokenness is simply the release of spiritual power, the Spirit doing his thing and power coming out. It happens only through brokenness, which I think is the most underrated virtue in the Christian community today. But beyond the release of power, there's this deep understanding of our weakness . . . It's a continually deepening revelation of your own impotence without the Spirit.[4]

As I read Crabb's words, I can't help but connect them to what the apostle Paul learned as he wrestled with the reality of his own weaknesses. After Paul had received what he describes as "surpassingly great revelations," he experienced a "thorn in the flesh." We don't know exactly what he was referring to, but we do know that he repeatedly received the same response from God as he prayed for the thorn to be removed. The Lord told him, "My grace is sufficient for you, for my power is made perfect in weakness." This led Paul to conclude, "For when I am weak, then I am strong" (2 Cor. 12:7–10).

Some people have misunderstood these verses and have misapplied them to their ministry endeavors, believing they should serve in areas where they are not passionate or gifted so that God can "use" their weakness. But the Bible makes it clear that God works through the passions and spiritual gifts He has placed in our lives. These verses say something about how God's power transforms us, not about how He empowers us to minister to others. It is when we are the weakest that God's power can truly transform us.

Power *in* before Power *to*

One of the greatest dangers associated with spiritual power is seen in those who exercise it without first having experienced God's transforming power. These religious power brokers know all the power plays; they are masters of rules, rituals, and organizational power games. But they lack the humility and brokenness necessary to enter into both an intimate relationship with God and loving relationships with others—a danger Jesus regularly confronted in the lives of the Pharisees, the religiously powerful of His day.

The Pharisees despised Jesus because He threatened their power base. The crowds recognized the power of Jesus when He taught "as One having authority" and performed miracles. Sensing that they were losing their grip on power, the Pharisees sought to undermine Jesus' credibility with such power plays as trick questions and trumped-up accusations that He had violated sacred traditions. Badgering Him constantly, the Pharisees tried to trick Jesus into making statements that would alienate a portion of the people who followed Him.

Jesus countered with a power play of His own. He engaged these religious power brokers in confrontation, answering their trick questions with equally confounding queries. He was not at all intimidated by these religious authorities, and He publicly identified them as hypocrites.

The conflict between Christ and the Pharisees illustrates the difference between wise and unwise stewardship of power. That contrast between the abuse of religious power, which is dysfunctional and destructive, and the right use of spiritual power, which is biblical and constructive, can be visualized using two pyramids.

The first pyramid illustrates how power is used naturally, apart from the transforming power of God. The progression illustrated by this pyramid can be seen in homes, workplaces, and churches, or any place power is used. The Pharisees displayed this abuse of power within the power structures of religion, but it can be displayed within family systems and corporate hierarchies as well.

Dysfunctional, Destructive Use of Power

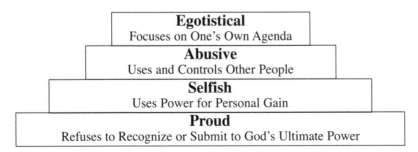

Egotistical
Focuses on One's Own Agenda

Abusive
Uses and Controls Other People

Selfish
Uses Power for Personal Gain

Proud
Refuses to Recognize or Submit to God's Ultimate Power

The second pyramid reflects the changed use of power that results when a person is increasingly transformed by the power of God's Spirit. Take a closer look at each of the pyramids. Which power pyramid best reflects the uses of power in your life? Your home? Your workplace? Your church?

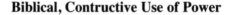

Biblical, Contructive Use of Power

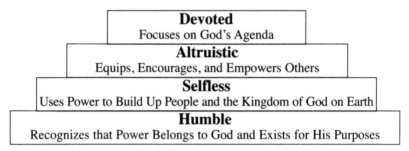

Devoted
Focuses on God's Agenda

Altruistic
Equips, Encourages, and Empowers Others

Selfless
Uses Power to Build Up People and the Kingdom of God on Earth

Humble
Recognizes that Power Belongs to God and Exists for His Purposes

Expression: God's Power *through* Me

God wants both to channel His power to us and to exercise His transforming power within us. But God's power play in the arena of the self doesn't end there. He does not intend for His power to be stored in us, as if we're some sort of spiritual battery. God wants to release His power through us to impact the lives of others. We make our greatest impact when we align ourselves with His inspiration and make ourselves completely available for His transformation. As we seek to influence others for their good and God's glory, we will begin to do the things that God is blessing rather than seeking to twist God's arm into blessing the things we feel like doing.

Power Received through Prayer

Prayer is fundamental to the expression of God's power through us. God made this clear to me in a dramatic way during my senior year of college. I had entered into a prayer pact with one of my best friends, Dennis Jackson. The two of us met for prayer each Friday at 6:00 a.m.—a great sacrifice for college students! Because I was approaching graduation, we consistently devoted a portion of our time to seeking God's will for the next step in my life.

Often when revealing His will to me, God begins broadly and then adds specificity to His leadings. With that in mind, Dennis and I prayed first as to whether I should go on to attend seminary or enter directly into ministry. God led me toward ministry. My friend and I then prayed about whether that ministry should be in a local church or in para-church setting. God led me toward the local church. Next we prayed about whether that should be an established church or a new congregation. God directed me toward church planting. Finally, Dennis and I sought God's leading concerning where that ministry should take place, and I felt directly led to Kentwood, Michigan. That is where the church I serve was planted in 1979. Having a clear sense that I have been aligned with God's purpose has sustained me through the ups and downs of ministry. I've enjoyed the confidence of knowing that it is God who provides the power I need for the purpose He has given.

God recently made the power of prayer clear to me again. Although God has consistently been gracious in giving me guidance in ministry over the years, there were two times when I sensed a dramatic "direct connect" with the will and power of God for my work. The first was when He called me to Kentwood as a senior in college, and the second was on Memorial Day of 2004. That day marked the twenty-fifth year that I had served as a pastor at Kentwood Community Church. I chose to devote the morning to prayer and journaling about my ministry. First I looked back, giving thanks to God for all His blessings and journaling about things I'd done in ministry that I would never want to repeat—mistakes from which God rescued me! Then I looked ahead to see what God might want to show me regarding my future ministry at Kentwood. I was a little nervous because a mentor of mine had recently given me this bit of advice: "You will know it's time to leave when you look back upon your ministry and much comes to mind, but then you look ahead and see a *blank screen!*"

As I began to seek God's leading, I remembered that when I first came to the church I had been greatly influenced by Laurel Buckingham. He had encouraged a number of us young pastors to seek a place of ministry where we could spend a lifetime. I had been thinking of a "lifetime" in terms of the biblical number of forty years. Having completed the first twenty-five years, I wondered if God would give me a clear vision for the next fifteen. Noticing the calendar year, I prayed, "Lord, can you give me *2020* vision?"

Far from imagining a blank screen, my mind was filled with dreams for the future. Over the next couple of hours, I felt that I was taking notes from God. My journal became filled with directions and dreams for the congregation at Kentwood Community Church—directions and dreams that would require all of us to completely depend upon Him and to offer our best to Him in order to make them a reality.

God had once again led me in a dramatic way through prayer.

Of course, I would never leave a time like that, no matter how moving the experience, and announce to the congregation that "God told me" what our ministry is to look like in the days ahead. Instead, I began sharing with trusted board members and staff members what I had experienced. As those plans resonated with them as being God's leading, I began to share the experience with a wider circle of leaders and, eventually, with the entire congregation. Together, we now see our mission clearly with the result that God is able to demonstrate his power through us.

Have you prayed about God's purpose for your life? Have you sought to describe what His will might look like in all the roles you fulfill at home, work, and church? The power of prayer is the power that comes from aligning our lives with His purposes.

Power through Gifts and Abilities

God empowers us not only through prayer but also through the strengths and spiritual gifts He has entrusted to us. Many wonderful books have been written on the subject of spiritual gifts and strengths. Reading any one of them provides a reminder that God has wired each of us in a specific way to make a difference in the lives of others. I have discovered that the more consistently I serve others according to God's design for my life, the more consistently I will experience His power working through me to impact others. In the words of John Maxwell, "God will regularly call you out of your comfort zone but rarely take you out of your gift zone."[5]

This does not mean that I let myself off the hook for certain character qualities because they are "not my gifts." While I have rarely scored high in the category of *showing mercy* (see Rom. 12:8) on a spiritual gifts inventory, it remains true that "blessed are the merciful, for they will be shown mercy" (Matt. 5:7). Nor does this mean that I can excuse myself from basic Christian responsibilities that I do not deem to be within my area of giftedness. The gift of evangelism is not one of my top three, but God still regularly arranges divine appointments in which I encounter others with whom he wants me to share His good news.

Two Dimensions of Power

Good stewardship of God-given power will cause power to flow in two directions. The stewardship of power has a vertical dimension, and it is called *worship*. Among other things, the act of worship is the recognition of God's power. In worship we sing timeless hymns like "All Hail the Power of Jesus' Name" and more recent choruses such as "Show Your Power" and "More Love, More Power." In doing so, we recognize that God is the source of power. The book of Revelation captures these expressions of worship in the heavenly realm, which repeatedly ascribe power to God:

You are worthy, our Lord and God, to receive glory and honor and *power*, for you created all things, and by your will they were created and have their being (Rev. 4:11, emphasis mine).

Worthy is the Lamb, who was slain, to receive *power* and wealth and wisdom and strength and honor and glory and praise (Rev. 5:12, emphasis mine).

To him who sits on the throne and to the Lamb be praise and honor and glory and *power*, for ever and ever! (Rev. 5:13, emphasis mine).

Amen! Praise and glory and wisdom and thanks and honor and *power* and strength be to our God for ever and ever. Amen! (Rev. 7:12, emphasis mine).

To worship is to recognize where power truly belongs and to submit to God's authority in all areas of life.

A second dimension to the good stewardship of power is horizontal. This dimension is called *witness,* and, among other things, it is the demonstration of God's power in our lives and in the world. To His disciples, Jesus promised, "But you will receive *power* when the Holy Spirit comes on you; and you will be my witnesses in Jerusalem, and in all Judea and Samaria, and to the ends of the earth" (Acts 1:8, emphasis mine). God always and only gives His power for His purposes. Witness demonstrates to others (and to ourselves) where power truly belongs and that the stewardship of that power remains under God's authority. Power expresses itself in both words and deeds, as does witness, resulting in appropriate influence in the lives of others.

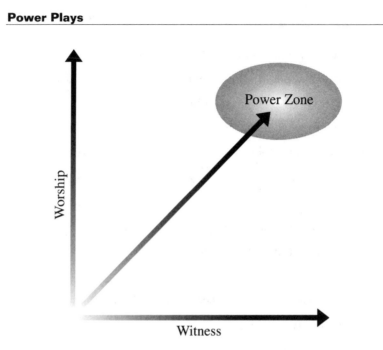

People who are the most powerless in their own right are often the most effective witnesses to God's power.

Purity and Power

A few years ago I was privileged to be part of a Christian history tour led by Dr. Jim Garlow in downtown Los Angeles. Jim guided us to the historic roots of two significant movements within Christianity—the Holiness movement and the Pentecostal movement. Both were born in the same places and among the same people, though the two movements soon separated. In comparing the two, our guide made a comment I'll never forget. He said, "The Holiness movement focused on the *purity* God's Spirit can provide; the Pentecostal movement focused more on the *power* of God's Spirit." As the tour concluded, our group prayed together. I remember asking God for *both* purity and power, convinced that one cannot be effective without the other.

This is the power of God for the arena of the self—power to transform both the human heart and, through those transformed individuals, to transform the world. It is this power that God wishes for every believer—a life of purity lived in the power that His Holy Spirit is fully capable to provide.

For Further Thought

1. As Ken discovered at the outset of this chapter, some Christians seem to expect too much from God while others expect too little. Why do you think that is?

2. What powers does God chooses to retain? Which does He choose to share? Why do you think He does that?

3. Read Ephesians 6. What are the power tools that Christians can use in order to withstand evil spiritual power? How do these tools function in your life?

4. Do you agree that God shares His power the most with those who are humble? How can you cultivate the virtue of humility in your life?

5. What is the relationship between power and pride? How have you seen this dynamic at work in your life?

6. What are the experiences—positive or negative—that have taught you the most about the stewardship of power?

7. Jesus set the principle that our faithfulness in handling small amounts of power will lead to opportunities for stewarding greater amounts of power. Can you give examples of how this principle has

worked in your life or the lives of others?

8. Conduct a personal inventory based on the Ten Commandments of Spiritual Authority. In which areas are you strongest? In which are you weakest? What action can you take to improve in each area?

9. What actions or experiences prompt you to expect more from God?

10. Examine the two power pyramids. Which pyramid best illustrates your current stewardship of power? How will your stewardship of power be affected by increasing the time and energy you devote to worship?

11. Which action of God's Spirit is most needed in your life — purity or power? What will you do to seek a greater measure of each?

The Power
to Love

Arena of Power:	Marriage
Source of Power:	Submission
Power Principle:	Control is the enemy of power.

Richard was at the very top of his professional life. The fifty-year-old lawyer had built a successful law firm around his formidable legal skills. As his practice grew, so did the number of employees who worked for him. His entrepreneurial leadership led to expanded responsibility in his profession—and an expanded investment portfolio. Richard felt truly power-full as his days were spent in the company of clients who respected his advice, employees who carried out his instructions, and vendors who catered to him because of his wealth.

Yet somewhere along the way, Richard's capacity for power began to shift from well-deserved to ill-managed. He began to believe that the power he had gained gave him the right to make demands not only in his professional life but also in his home and neighborhood. This sense of power, fueled by some personal and emotional difficulties, subtly changed how Richard related to others—especially those closest to him.

Richard's dysfunctional exercise of power had inflated his ego until he saw himself as the center of his universe. He began to believe that he brought everything to his marriage while his wife contributed nothing. In condescending ways, he began to let her know that she ought to be grateful to be married to him and that without him, her life would be aimless and miserable.

In reality, this abuse of power in Richard's marriage was the very source of his wife's misery. She was a capable person who would have been far from helpless without him. As she began to set the boundaries that produce a healthy relationship, Richard's anger and abuse of power became more dramatic. He began to use the power tools that erode trust and intimacy in a marriage. When unable to get his way, he delivered an intimidating silent treatment. When that power tool didn't produce results, he resorted to verbal abuse, including the use of language that clearly violated his Christian convictions. One day Richard resorted to abusing his wife physically, and his longsuffering but courageous wife appropriately drew the line.

By God's grace, Richard began to see what he had become and to realize the impact his power plays had had on his marriage. He intentionally began to seek ways in which he could serve and encourage his partner, and his relapses into the abuse of power became less frequent. As Richard began to use his God-given power to build up his wife, their marriage was healed and grew stronger.

For many people, marriage is the first test of their use of power. In this arena, more so than any other, the wills of two human beings can come into conflict. The first resort for most people is to exert the will, using power to control their partner. The result is conflict.

In reality, it is the surrender of control that leads to the greatest power of all, the power to love. Jesus said, "For whoever wants to save his life will lose it, but whoever loses his life for me and for the gospel will save it" (Mark 8:35). When we willingly sacrifice our lives, we do not lose. When we surrender ourselves and honor our partner, we gain greater power—that is, a greater ability to turn our intentions into action.

A Power-Full Arrangement

If power is the capacity to turn intention into action, then every marriage is a relationship laden with opportunities to exercise power. The marriage ceremony itself includes a declaration of intent. Both parties express the intention to receive the other as husband or wife. Those intentions are further clarified by the making of a vow—an affirmation that whatever the circumstances ("for better, for worse; for richer, for poorer; in sickness and in health") the partners will love and cherish each other. The marriage ceremony has long been recognized as a commitment of love and faith. It should also be seen as a commitment to the proper stewardship of power within the most intimate of relationships.

One aspect of marriage that makes it a power-full arrangement is its exclusivity. In marriage, two people make themselves vulnerable to each other, pledging that some of their deepest needs will be met only in the context of their relationship. Forsaking all others, the two depend only on their spouses for certain dimensions of personal fulfillment. Within that context of vulnerability and exclusivity, a good steward of power—someone who purposefully turns the intentions expressed in the marriage ceremony into action—is a tremendous blessing to a spouse. Likewise, a poor steward of power—one who ignores the intentions expressed in the marriage vows or, worse yet, exploits the vulnerability of a spouse—can make marriage the most difficult of relationships. Marriage will test one's use of power.

I often tell people that the greatest challenge of marriage isn't discovering the identity of your spouse but discovering your own character. I learned that from experience! Early in my own marriage, my personal insecurities began to emerge. These insecurities had always been present in my life, but the depth of relationship experienced in marriage brought these long-buried tendencies to the surface. The way I compensated for my insecurities was by resorting to a power tool; I used my power as a husband in an attempt to control my wife. These attempts at control brought little relief from my insecurities and only stifled the development of our relationship. One day while reading, I came across this statement, which God used to deeply convict me of this misuse of power: The greatest enemy of intimacy is control. I recognized the truth of that statement immediately and have seen it played out both positively and negatively in my own marriage and those of others. The more we seek to control a person, the less likely we will be able to experience significant intimacy with that person. When I realized that I was being a poor steward of power in my marriage, I began to shift my energy away from activities intended to control my wife into activities that would nurture our relationship. It worked. I happily discovered that the intimacy gained from building up my mate quickly overpowered my own insecurities.

The use of power is an often-overlooked dynamic in both premarital and marital counseling. To be successful in creating a marriage, couples must grasp the power dynamics within their relationship and see how their use of power compares or contrasts with what God desires. As Richard Foster says in his book *Money, Sex, and Power*, "If money hits us in the pocketbook, and sex hits us in the bedroom, power hits us in our relationships. Power profoundly impacts our interpersonal relationships, our social relationships, and our relationship with God. Nothing touches us more profoundly for good or for ill than power."[1]

The right use of power turns our best intentions into consistent actions that develop the marriage relationship. Wrongly used, power can destroy the trust and intimacy of a marriage. It was the abuse of power that led to the destruction of the very first marriage relationship—the one between Adam and Eve. Again, Foster writes (emphasis mine),

Think of Adam and Eve in the garden—given every pleasure, every delight, everything necessary for a good life. Yet they wanted more; they grasped and grabbed in a headlong rush to be like God, to know good and evil. *The sin of the garden was the sin of power.* They wanted to be more, to have more, to know more than is right. Not content to be creatures, they wanted to be gods.[2]

This power play ruptured first their relationship with God and then their relationship with each other.

The Power to Serve

Two forms of power are particularly worthy of focus in the arena of marriage. The first is the power to serve—utilizing the capacity for power provided by the intimacy of marriage to meet a spouse's needs rather than seeking to meet our own. There are two obstacles to the correct use of power in this area: ignorance and selfishness. So our capacity to exercise the power to serve can be increased by addressing two questions:

- Do I know what my spouse needs?
- Am I willing to meet those needs?

If I don't know what my spouse needs, then I will be unable to serve my partner, no matter how willing I may be. On the other hand, if I know what my spouse needs but am unwilling to meet those needs, my knowledge will be useless at best and dangerous at worst. Every time I know my spouse's needs and meet them, I fill the reservoir of our relationship. Each time I fail to meet my partner's needs, I drain from the reservoir. All of us occasionally do one or the other. It is not a single action of serving or failing to serve but a consistent pattern of either servanthood or selfishness that makes or breaks a marriage. When we consistently serve our spouse, our relationship brims with intimacy, love, and trust. When we consistently drain those resources by acting selfishly, the marriage suffers.

Servanthood

Selfishness

The Power of Knowing: The Husband

Knowing what my spouse needs eliminates the barrier of ignorance. Whoever coined the phrase "Ignorance is bliss" certainly knew nothing about marriage. Marriage partners come together as individuals with distinct histories, tastes, knowledge sets, preferences, and needs. Even after a period of courtship, they may be largely ignorant of each other's deepest needs. In addition, partners often have the tendency to project their own needs onto each other. The husband, for example, may assume that he knows what his wife wants emotionally, financially, or sexually, because he desires it himself. In reality, the needs of a man and a woman in marriage are often quite different. It is true, isn't it, that opposites attract.

While it really does take a lifetime to fully know the needs of another person, there are some common needs shared by most men and women. In his book *His Needs, Her Needs,* marriage counselor Willard F. Harley Jr. identifies the top five needs of a typical husband and the top five needs of a typical wife.[3] The comments on Dr. Harley's categories are mine, based on the things I'm learning as I seek to be a good steward of power in meeting my wife's needs. First, let's consider the needs of a typical husband.

1. Sexual Fulfillment. Sexual fulfillment is the primary relational need for a typical married man. Unfortunately, many churches tend to make men feel guilty about this. Perhaps we've forgotten that the sexual relationship was God's idea and that, in spite of the world's distortion of sexuality, it remains part of God's design for a strong and healthy marriage.

It is true that for many men, the saturation of our culture with sexual stimulants has created an unhealthy and inappropriate focus on this need. A husband must monitor his sexual desires to be sure that they reflect God's healthy design and not the world's distorted image of it. A man must guard his eyes against the pornography that is so readily available today. Men, we must realize that the world has inflated this legitimate need until it has become an illegitimate lust that no woman could ever satisfy. At the same time, we must be honest about our strong need for sexual fulfillment. Many of the Christian men that I know admit that this need remains strong and consistent even within the careful boundaries they have set for themselves to avoid inappropriate visual stimulation. Sexual fulfillment within marriage meets this important need and, therefore, deepens the intimacy of the relationship—not just physically but emotionally and spiritually as well.

2. Recreational Companionship. It might be said that the couple who *plays* together stays together. Typically, a husband deeply appreciates a wife's interest in his recreational pursuits. I was grateful when my wife, Jan, took up running a few years ago and participated in some five-kilometer events with me. I enjoy our annual getaway at Christmastime to enjoy some snowshoeing. Jan even attends a football game with me once in a while! Her interest in my interests has been empowering for me.

3. An Attractive Spouse. Physical appearance is one of the first things that attracts potential mates to each other, and it remains an important element in a relationship even after marriage. Men, in particular, wish for their partners to be physically attractive. While this may be a legitimate need on the part of a husband, there is a danger that he may set unrealistically high standards of appearance for his partner. Many wives, too, place unreasonable expectations upon themselves in this area. Even supermodels aren't that super all the time and appear as they do largely because of the the manipulations of photographers and graphic designers. Maybe the best definition of attractiveness is this one: doing your best with what you have.

When dating, most women give extra attention to their appearance, taking their future husband's tastes in hairstyle, clothing, and makeup into account. Unfortunately, many women give too little attention to their appearance—and to their husband's preference for their appearance—after marriage. If it is true that many men must be less critical of their partner's appearance, releasing them from the unhealthy and unrealistic expectations set by popular culture, it is equally true that many women should give greater attention to satisfying their husband's needs in this area, recognizing that their appearance sends a powerful message to their mate about how much he is valued.

A young woman in our church shared this incident with me. One day she decided to forego the ritual of putting on makeup, remaining dressed in an old sweat suit. She reasoned that since she had no plans to go out and expected no one to drop by, her appearance wouldn't matter. When her husband came home that afternoon, he wisely said nothing, but she perceived his attitude from the look in his eyes. Without thinking, she commented defensively: "I knew I wasn't going to see anyone today, so I didn't bother getting dressed." Instantly the message she had sent to her husband dawned on her: "You weren't anybody worth bothering for." That is the message a wife can convey if she doesn't seek to remain attractive to her husband.

4. Domestic Support. While role expectations have shifted a good deal in marriage over the past generation, husbands continue to have an expectation that their wives play a role in making the home a sanctuary for the family. This doesn't mean a husband can or should expect his wife to do all the work in maintaining a household. Like many women, my wife has a fulltime career. We divide household chores between us so that we have equal responsibility both inside and outside the home. Yet Jan contributes something more than I do, making our home a retreat for our family—and for her husband in particular. What makes a home a great place for a husband to be may be different for every man and every house. For me, my wife accomplishes this wonderfully by providing protection from inappropriate intrusions. She's usually the one to answer the door or the phone. She is very good at discerning which callers I would welcome and which are unnecessary or annoying. This is a wonderful form of domestic support.

5. Admiration. Men have a basic need to be respected by others, and that begins at home. Behind every great husband is a wife who respects and admires him. The Spirit of God often seeks to channel affirmation to a husband through his wife. A wife who affirms her husband creates a stronger man, one better able to meet her needs.

How well do you know your husband's needs? While the needs listed here are typical, they may not be the needs of your husband—or his may be in a different priority. One way to find out is to go on a *discussion date.* A discussion date is held in a setting conducive to personal conversation between husband and wife, such as a coffee shop, restaurant, or walk around the neighborhood. On that date, ask questions like these:

- Are the needs stated in this book the same as yours? Did this author get them right? Would you state them differently?
- How would you rank your needs? Which are most important to you? Which are least important?

- How am I doing in meeting your needs? Which do I meet consistently? Is there any area in which I could improve at giving you what you need?

Don't miss this important consideration: the focus of the wife should be on her *husband's* needs. Husbands, it is an illegitimate use of power to be preoccupied with your own needs, even the legitimate needs listed above. A wife should focus on meeting the needs of her husband, and a husband should focus on meeting the needs that follow.

The Power of Knowing: The Wife

It will come as no surprise that the top five needs of most wives are different than those of their husbands. The typical wife's five basic needs in marriage are as follows—again, my comments are added to the basic categories drawn from Dr. Harley's work.

1. Affection. Affection is the wife's greatest need, and it can be met in a number of ways. A husband can express affection through physical touch, notes, gifts, phone calls, opening doors, or asking his wife out on a date. Affection is the glue in a marriage relationship. While husbands typically have a greater desire for sex, their wives may more often crave simple affection.

Men, the excuse "I'm just not that affectionate" simply will not cut it. Affection is not a temperament trait that some people simply do not have. Affection is a powerful connection with one's wife, and every husband must develop the capacity to express it. That can be done by cultivating habits such as exchanging a hug and a kiss each morning, saying "I love you" before leaving the house, talking by phone during the day, sharing an embrace upon returning home, and spending a few minutes talking about how *her* day went. These are things every husband can do, whether he sees himself as the affectionate type or not.

Sometimes even silly things can be powerful conveyors of affection. Every so often I buy several packs of my wife's favorite gum and hide them throughout our bedroom and bathroom. She jokingly notes that the "gum fairy" has struck again, but the unexpected discovery of a pack of gum tucked away in a drawer affectionately communicates to her that she has been on my mind. That knowledge empowers her to invest herself in meeting my needs in return.

A word of caution is in order here. Husbands, take note: being a good steward of your power to serve requires that you meet your wife's number one need selflessly—that is, without a hidden agenda to get your number one need met in return. It is a mistake to display affection to your spouse only as a prelude to sexual intimacy. To do so communicates precisely the opposite message that you intend; it tells your partner that she is of value only sexually. Nonsexual touch is a skill that all husbands can and should learn.

2. Conversation. Husbands discover a tremendous source of power when they give to their wives the gift of undivided attention. Jan and I go on a date nearly every week. We define a date as an activity that includes time alone in a setting conducive to conversation. Although we enjoy going out with other couples, we do not count that as a date. Likewise, we enjoy taking in a movie now and then; but if all we do is sit side by side staring at the screen, we don't

65

count that evening as a date. It is the opportunity for conversation—including both speaking and listening—that makes the activity a date and meets her need for conversation (and mine also).

3. Honesty and Openness. Prenuptial agreements have grown in popularity as a means of ensuring that certain conditions will be met, especially in the case of divorce. Honesty, however, is a much better "insurance policy" for a marriage. Many husbands lie to their wives or withhold parts of their lives from them.

There are at least three types of liars when it comes to marriage. The first is a *pattern liar.* This is a husband for whom lying is a way of life. It was his coping mechanism long before he met his wife, and he brings this power tool into the marriage with him. For the pattern liar, lying is a life habit, a manifestation of an ingrained pattern of the flesh that has not been rooted out by God's Spirit. The second type of liar is a *pressure liar.* This is a husband who is honest most of the time but who lies when he feels cornered by a problem. The third type of liar is the *protective liar.* This is a husband who believes that the truth will be too much for his wife to bear, so he "protects" her by hiding his true feelings or the depths of problems that potentially threaten their relationship.

During the process of adopting our daughter, I unexpectedly discovered that I had become a protective liar. Expanding our family through adoption has been one of the greatest blessings of our lives, but initially my wife was much more enthusiastic about the idea than I was. During a counseling session that was required to complete the adoption process, I was confronted by the counselor about my true feelings. He rightly discerned that I wasn't sharing some of my thoughts with Jan and challenged me about it. Subsequently, I've become much more open with my wife about my feelings, even when I know they will initially make her uncomfortable. That honesty and openness has deepened our relationship.

4. Financial Support. Although many families now depend upon two incomes, wives generally view their husband as primarily responsible for supporting the family financially. In the same way that husbands must be careful to ensure that their expectation for their wife's attractiveness is realistic, wives must be sure their expectation of financial support from their husband is appropriate. If husbands sometimes have an unattainable ideal of physical perfection in mind for their wife, wives can hold to an ideal of financial security or lavish spending that their husband cannot ultimately provide. In this regard, the cultivation of contentment can prevent the development of resentment. That being said, a wife is blessed by a husband who devotes himself to supporting the family financially and ensuring important financial goals of the household are met. In this sense, a husband is not only a provider of income but a provider in meeting one of the most common needs of a wife—security.

Meeting a wife's need for support goes beyond providing money and includes inviting her participation in financial decisions. In many households, even if it is the wife who actually pays the bills and balances the checkbook, the responsibility for making major decisions about money rests with the husband. In general, men more so than women are comfortable with assuming the role of chief decision maker and having primary control over family finances. Very often, men will make buying decisions, even about large purchases, on their own, without consulting their wives. Women, on the other hand, tend to prefer consulting with their mate about buying decisions because it reinforces a sense of togetherness. Author Olivia Mellan offers this advice, "When you look at the conflicts with your partner over money, you need to determine whether there is a large power imbalance as far as controlling the money is concerned. If either one of you feels uncomfortable about this imbalance, try to move toward a more democratic distribution of power."[4]

5. *Family Commitment.* The husband who is committed to being a good father and is both interested in and investing in his children meets important needs for them and for his wife. Parenting takes time and training, and a husband who makes both a priority exercises the power of serving in his marriage.

How well do you know your wife? Are the needs listed here also her top five? Would she prioritize them in this order? Invite your wife on a discussion date and find out. Ask her questions like these:

- Are the needs stated in this book the same as yours? Did this author get them right? Would you state them differently?
- How would you rank your needs? Which are most important to you? Which are least important?
- How am I doing in meeting your needs? Which do I meet consistently? Is there any area in which I could improve at giving you what you need?
- After asking each question, listen non-defensively and allow plenty of time for her to reply.

The Power of the Will

Our first question, "Do I know what my spouse needs?" addressed the barrier of ignorance. This second question, "Am I willing to meet those needs?" gets at the barrier of selfishness.

Selfishness is a deeper issue than ignorance is. We can turn to Christian counselors for a practical understanding of human needs. But to overcome the barrier of selfishness and consistently set aside our own desires in order to meet the needs of another, we must turn to the powerful Word of God and Spirit of God. Overcoming selfishness takes self-control, self-denial, and a healthy self-esteem in the most biblical sense: loving your neighbor as yourself (see Mark 12:31). Richard Foster notes, "In the individual, power is to be used to promote self-control, not self-indulgence. Self-control is at home with both self-esteem and self-denial . . . Self-denial is the way the human hunger for self-esteem is satisfied, and self-control embraces them both."[5]

Meeting needs is an act of servanthood because it requires us to give to others in ways that seem alien to us—we don't necessarily experience or appreciate the needs of our spouse. We must learn to understand our spouse as a person totally different from ourselves. The differences identified between men and women by the priority of their top five needs make it difficult for the two sexes to naturally empathize with and appreciate the other's needs. As married people, we, by faith, meet needs that we do not feel ourselves.

The Power of Submission. Ephesians 5:21–33 is a classic text that challenges husbands and wives to move beyond selfishness to develop a relationship that reflects the relationship Christ has with His bride, the church. The passage begins by making it clear that the power to over-come selfishness, the capacity to turn our good intentions into action, is not humanly generated. That capacity to serve—and especially to serve one's spouse in marriage—is Spirit generated. Ephesians 5:21 commands us to "submit to one another out of reverence for Christ." The verb *submit* (5:21) is in sequence with several previous verbs, including *speak, sing*, and *give thanks* (5:19–20), all of which result from obeying the command "be filled with the Spirit" (5:18). If we rely on our own will in order to accomplish this, ingrained flesh patterns will lead us back into selfish ways of having our own needs met. The flesh will never mesh, as the saying goes. Or, expressed in biblical terms, we will not know the reality of two becoming one flesh. But when relying on the Spirit, we receive the capacity not only to meet our spouse's needs but also to meet them joyfully, not in the drudgery of fulfilling a mere duty.

This Spirit-generated capacity to submit ourselves to meeting the needs of another positions us both to give to our spouses *and* to receive from them. Foster states it well:

Submission is power because it places us in a position in which we can receive from others. We are impoverished people indeed if our world is narrowed down to ourselves. But when, with humility of heart, we submit to others, vast new resources are opened up to us. When we submit to others, we have access to their wisdom, their counsel, their rebuke, their encouragement.[6]

In order to experience this capacity to serve, we must set for ourselves the priority revealed in Ephesians 5: having reverence for Christ. This healthy configuration for marriage is often pictured as a triangle with Christ at the pinnacle and the husband and wife at opposite corners of the

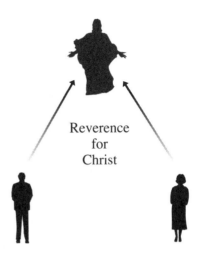

Reverence
for
Christ

base. As both husband and wife move toward the top of the triangle—having reverence for Christ—they draw closer to one another.

There is another way of utilizing this familiar concept to illustrate the power to serve. In meeting each other's needs, a husband and wife don't merely focus on each other, drawing from their own energy to meet each other's needs in a horizontal direction. As the partners ascend

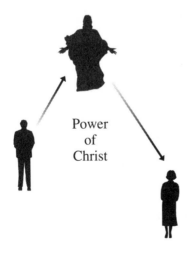

Power
of
Christ

the triangle in reverence to Christ, they receive power through His Spirit and are enabled to meet their partner's needs. In this way, as we reverence Christ, His power flows down the triangle on our spouse's side, increasing his or her capacity to serve.

How, then, do marriage partners show reverence for

Christ? One way that I reverence Christ each day is through prayer. Prayer empowers me to transcend my selfishness and serve my spouse. During my devotional time each morning, I pray for Jan and for our marriage. As I reflect upon our marriage while praying, the Spirit prompts me and empowers me to fulfill my highest intentions for my marriage relationship.

Submission by the Wife. Ephesians 5 describes two primary ways a wife expresses her part in the mutual submission of husband and wife. The first is by yielding her right to function as and focus only on herself as an individual. It's an act of servanthood to yield one's rights rather than to be preoccupied with and insist upon claiming one's rights. The yielding of rights, then, is not a matter of inferiority but humility. And there is an important condition to this yielding: it is to be done "as to the Lord," a disclaimer against any yielding that may involve sinful activity.

The second way a wife expresses her part in mutual submission is by respecting her husband (5:33). *Respect* is a strong word and is in fact the same word earlier rendered as *reverence* directed to Christ (5:21). Respect carries with it both the notion of respecting one's husband as a person and the notion of respecting his position of leadership in the home. Respect is to be given even at times when it is not earned. Through respect, a wife may well inspire her husband to live and lead at a higher level. One wife reported, after reading a book that convinced her that she should serve her husband, "He became the man I believed he could be."

Submission by the Husband. Ephesians 5 also describes two primary ways a husband expresses his part in the mutual submission of a married couple. The first is through sacrificial love (5:25). While Paul's teaching

72

on the subject of submission by wives would have been expected in the culture of his day, his challenge for husbands to sacrificially love their wives would have come as a complete shock. The social mores of the first century would have advised, "Husbands, rule your wives," not "Husbands, love your wives." Paul commands Christian husbands to use their power within their families not to rule but to love. This love, powerfully modeled by Christ, is not based on an external cause but on internal character. Loving as Christ loved does not depend on what others are doing—including the spouse—but entirely upon what Christ has done in our hearts when we invite Him to work in us. Our example is Christ, who gave himself up for His bride, the Church. The axiom that we "give up to go up" is true not only in leadership but in marriage as well. If a husband is willing to sacrifice his life for his wife, he will be willing to make lesser sacrifices also. He will be willing to put his own likes, desires, opinions, and preferences aside when doing so will best meet the needs of his partner. The second way a husband expresses his part in mutual submission is through sanctifying love (Eph. 5:26–33). When husbands love their wives as Christ loved the Church, it is cleansing, not condemning. While we should never settle for sin or sinful patterns in our mate (or in ourselves), our relationship with our partner should be redemptive and not condemning. Our love should communicate that we want the best for the one loved and cannot bear for her to be corrupted or misled by anything harmful. Just as taking proper care of our own body strengthens it, so the proper care for our spouse strengthens her and the marriage relationship.

Love is the first mark of the proper stewardship of power. Richard Foster states, "Love demands that power be used for the good of others. Notice Jesus' use of power—the healing of the blind, the sick, the maimed, the dumb, the leper and many others ... In Christ, power is used to destroy the evil so that love can redeem the good."[7] As husbands love their wives in sacrificial and sanctifying ways, the evil that threatens their marriages is thwarted, and even the difficult experiences of marriage can be redemptive.

Husband ←——— mutual submission ———→ **Wife**

Sacrificing love   Submission

Sanctifying love   Respect

The Power of Mutual Submission. The ultimate goal of marriage is not happiness but holiness. While God desires for us to experience joy and fulfillment in marriage, His primary concern is that our stewardship of power in marriage should make us more like Him. A study published in *Time* magazine attempted to identify life experiences that produce lasting happiness. The study found that while the initial days of marriage temporarily elevate a person's level of happiness, it soon returns to whatever level of happiness that the person experienced previous to marriage. The study reported also that owning a pet is one of the greatest producers of happiness among those people who wanted a pet.[8] With tongue in cheek, I conclude that if you're interested only in happiness, don't get married—buy a dog!

More seriously, the study illustrates the truth that if I enter marriage focusing primarily on my own happiness, I will likely be preoccupied with my own needs. However, if I enter marriage with a primary focus on becoming a more holy person, it is more likely that I will give reverence to Christ and, in the process, will utilize my Spirit-given capacity to serve my spouse's needs. When it comes to meeting needs, many couples adopt the philosophy embodied in this saying: "I'll meet you half way, baby; that's better than no way." I've heard couples quote that statement as if it were a Bible verse. In reality, it is a bargaining chip for marital power plays. Many couples consider marriage to be a 50/50 proposition. But there are certain to be times when a spouse is capable of giving only 20 percent. Unexpected job demands, physical or mental illness, or a host of other problems can affect a partner's ability to contribute to the marriage. If the other partner is determined to give 50 percent and no more, there will be a shortfall.

Marriage isn't a 50/50 proposition. Both husband and wife must give 100 percent. Each partner is empowered by the Spirit to follow the example of Christ—and He gave it all. If you are committed to giving 100 percent and your spouse is able to give only 20 percent, your marriage can survive—and even thrive—because of your sacrificial giving.

When husband and wife know each other's needs and are empowered by the Spirit to meet those needs, they develop the power to serve. As they choose to exercise that power, they will move beyond the obstacles of ignorance and selfishness to develop the life-long relationship of intimacy that marriage is intended to be.

The Power to Stay

The second form of power that is essential for the good stewardship of power in the arena of marriage is the power to stay, or what the Bible describes as the power of perseverance. Any relationship will be tested by trials and temptations, and this is certainly true of marriage. Many couples mistakenly believe that when difficulties come, it is an indication either that they've married the wrong person or that the marriage couldn't possibly develop the depth of intimacy that God intended. But staying power, or perseverance, makes it possible to experience the meaning on the other side of the misery.

The Trajectory of Perseverance

Rather than seeing difficult times as a death knell for a marriage, it is better to view them as a necessary and likely unavoidable phase in the development of an enduring, intimate relationship. Many years ago Anne and Ray Ortlund concluded, "Every undertaking in your life incorporates three periods of time. Recognize when you're in each one, follow certain principles prescribed for each, and God will bring you through."[9] They described these zones as follows.

A Zone—Desire to Achieve. This zone is characterized by idealism, even naïveté, and perhaps also apprehension. The attitude toward the future is marked by hope for success. This is the honey-moon period, where love is real but yet to mature. The atmosphere is romantic and exciting, and the partner is idealized. Commitment is untested and conflicts are avoided.

Jan and I were married when she was nineteen and I was twenty-one. We don't necessarily recommend marriage at this youthful age to others, but it was quite common in the religious subculture we grew up in. If you had asked us on our wedding day about the depth of our love, we would have enthusiastically responded that we could have imagined no deeper love than what we were experiencing. We knew little about the demands of marriage, but hoped for much from it.

B Zone—Desire to Quit. This zone is characterized by confusion and conflict. The attitude toward the future is marked by uncertainty. Disappointments and disillusionment may come because of the partner's failures and limitations. Marital stress increases due to the discovery of differences between the couple, money problems, child raising, fatigue, and misunderstandings. Hope may begin to fade. Commitment is uncertain. Conflicts are constant. This is the danger zone.

The B Zone ends in one of two ways. Either (1) the couple quits the marriage, and in the aftermath, problems remain unsolved. Emotional baggage piles up, including negative memories, wounds, scars, and self-doubts. The attitude toward the future is marked by fear, timidity, and a tendency to be overcautious. This creates uncertainty not only for the two marriage partners but also for generations to come. Unresolved problems are carried into the next relationship and into the lives of children.

Or (2) the couple perseveres in their marriage, and God causes the C Zone to emerge. It is important to recognize that trusting God in the B Zone and attempting to persevere doesn't mean that change will come quickly. Sometimes our faith reaches out to God just as He is on the verge of changing a difficult situation. At other times, God intends to change the situation but at a later time. Still, at other times, the situation may not change during our lifetime. The Ortlunds offer these words of hope: "God will never let a B Zone last too long—even if it ends in death, from eternity's viewpoint, it wasn't too long."[10]

C Zone—Achievement, Maintenance, Growth. This zone is characterized by personal satisfaction, a sense of realism, maturity, and perspective. Skills have been developed to deal with the future B Zones. The attitude toward the future is one of optimism, courage, and the expectation of success. What the married couple experiences is no longer a puppy love but a deep love that is hard to explain. The couple is not totally free of frustrations but no longer doubts that the marriage will succeed.

Tragically, many people never get to experience the depth of love found in the C Zone. Any marriage that is terrific today was not so terrific at some earlier point. The couple is now experiencing the benefit of the power to stay, perseverance. That power is not self-generated. In the words of James M. Baird Jr., "Our perseverance is really His perseverance in us." Lewis Smedes also reminds us of the staying power required to prevail in marriage:

Committed love does not say "finish" before the last act is played out. It gives us the strength to tough out bad times in hope of better times. Committed love does not throw in the towel before the fight is really over. It holds on. And while it holds, it energizes, it gives you strength to keep the door open for the day when a new beginning may be possible.[11]

This staying power, along with the serving power of committed love, creates a God-honoring legacy. When we exercise these powers in tandem—the power to serve and the power to stay—we not only create a deep marriage relationship but also reap the character qualities in ourselves that come by perseverance—and the eternal reward that awaits us in the life to come.

Developing Staying Power

Some who are reading these words are in a B Zone right now, or soon will be. So the question of developing staying power will be an urgent one for some. Where does staying power come from? In order to exercise staying power in marriage, we must first exhibit perseverance in relationship with God. Jesus commanded us to A.S.K. in prayer: Ask. Seek. Knock. He told the parable of the persistent widow to remind us that we should always pray and never give up. Staying power begins with prayer.

Facing Conflict Early. Then, staying power must be focused on the problems that can undermine a marriage. The earlier those conflicts are faced, the better. If conflicts are serious enough to threaten a marriage relationship, they will only escalate with the passing of time. That escalation of conflict can be envisioned in this way:

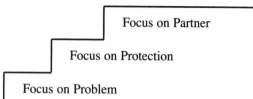

Focus on Partner

Focus on Protection

Focus on Problem

When a conflict develops and a couple addresses it early, there is the opportunity to focus on the real problem or source of conflict. Working together on fixing the problem, the two will rationally discuss what is wrong and what can be done to remedy it. Their use of language will be clear, specific, and oriented to the here and now, not loaded with innuendo or blaming. The pair will have a common goal to diagnose the source, not just the symptoms, of the conflict. Those sources may be interpersonal (having to do with each other), intrapersonal (located within one of the partners), or substantive (concerning external issues). In the language of Ephesians 4, at this level the couple will be speaking the truth in love and saying what benefits the other.

If the conflict is not addressed or resolved at this level, it can escalate to the next where the focus will be on self-protection. One or both of the marriage partners will be less concerned with problem solving than with protecting their own interests. A new concern enters the discussion—the self. Both partners will still want to solve the problem but will also want to come out of the conflict looking good. Their communication will become more general, making it harder to identify the source of the problem.

When a conflict escalates to its highest level, the focus shifts to the partner. This is a shift from self-protection to winning. Communication becomes distorted, issues are magnified, the partners become polarized, and over-generalization characterizes their conversations ("You always . . ." or "You never . . ."), which are riddled with assumptions and irrational thinking. In the language of Ephesians 4, those involved are filled with anger. They are no longer speaking the truth but lying, and they are using words that tear down each other. Within this level of conflict, there are degrees of destructive behavior.

- Concentration on Winning—Each partner wants to win and for the other to lose.
- Concentration on Hurting—Partners say or do things to wound each other.
- Concentration on Destroying—Partners seek to hurt each other in ways that will make it impossible to fully recover.

I have seen couples allow their unresolved conflict to escalate to the point that their sole purpose in life was to take revenge on each other. This leads to separation or divorce at the very least, and sometimes to an ongoing war that uses the courtroom as its arena and children as the weapon. I have also seen couples recognize that their conflict was escalating and humbly submit themselves to a process of resolution that included godly counsel. Thankfully, I have seen many such couples who now know the joy of a relationship where new conflicts are faced early and resolved completely.

Guidelines for Conflict Resolution. One of the most practical and powerful guides to resolving conflict is found in Ephesians 4.

From this passage, I draw a top ten list of conflict resolution principles:

1. Be humble, gentle, and patient (4:2).
2. Value unity (4:3).
3. Speak the truth in love (4:15, 25).
4. Relate to each other with new attitudes and actions (4:23–24), putting off old, unproductive styles that are more about meeting selfish needs than strengthening the relationship.
5. Deal with unresolved anger (4:26, 30–31).
6. Guard against unwholesome talk (4:29).
7. Seek to build the other up (4:29).
8. Build the other up according to their needs (4:29).
9. Be forgiving (4:32).
10. Behave as Christ did (4:32), remembering that His example—not our feelings or the behavior of our partner—is our standard.

Ephesians 4 is a wonderful text for couples to study together. Remember that God's Word is *active* (Heb. 4:12). It has the necessary energy to effect change even in the middle of conflict. Let His Word convict you about ways you need to handle conflict more appropriately, and let it comfort you when you've done your best without seeing the results you had hoped for.

The Power to Love

Most of us enter marriage with the attitude that Richard displayed at the outset of this chapter. We believe that we must control our partner in order to gain satisfaction. Nothing could be further from the truth. The fact is that the more we attempt to exercise power *over* our mate, the more frustrating and unsatisfying the relationship becomes. There is no power in seeking to control others. The best—and the only successful—use of power in the arena of marriage is the power the builds up our mate. By serving our mate—setting our own needs aside and lovingly meeting the needs of our spouse—and by persevering—focusing our energies on solving conflicts rather than protecting ourselves or attacking our partner—we discover the true power in the most basic and most intimate relationship of our lives. We discover the power to love.

For Further Thought

1. Why is marriage such a power-charged relationship?

2. The author makes the case that the greatest enemy of intimacy is control. Do you agree? Why or why not?

3. If you are married, can you name occasions when either ignorance or selfishness formed a barrier to growth in your marriage? If you are not married, can you name occasions when these obstacles have hampered the development of other kinds of relationships?

4. List some of the questions that you would ask your spouse on a discussion date.

5. How would you respond to each of the questions listed in this chapter if your spouse were to ask them of you during a discussion date?

6. What is the difference between exercising power for self-control and for self-indulgence? How are the two uses of power the same? How are they different?

7. Relate a time when your spouse expressed a need that you did not understand. Were you able to meet that need regardless of the fact that you didn't share it? What was the result?

8. The author makes the case that submitting oneself to a spouse actually strengthens rather than weakens both the marriage and the individual who has submitted. Do you agree?

9. The author names prayer as one action that helps a partner submit to his or her spouse. Can you name other actions that might help in developing mutual submission?

10. When you were first married, were you focused more on happiness or holiness? Has your focus shifted at all since then?

11. This chapter identifies three zones of conflict in marriage, the A, B, and C Zones. Have you experienced these zones in your marriage? What was the result?

12. Conduct a self-inventory using the ten conflict resolution principles as a guide. Which of these principles do you apply well? Which do you do poorly? What action will you take to improve your conflict resolution skills?

The Power to Change

Arena of Power: Family

Source of Power: Awareness

Power Principle: I can exercise power only in
the present, not in the past.

Bob calls it a "short fuse." Although he is usually a gentle, soft-spoken man with an easy smile, Bob is given to fits of anger, most frequently directed toward his children. The thirty-six-year-old schoolteacher is a devoted father who loves his kids and makes the time to show it. But too often his discipline comes as an explosion of rage rather than a thoughtful expression of boundaries and consequences.

Deep down, Bob knows that his outbursts of anger make his children angry as well. As the children have grown into young teenagers, they have begun to display this same short fuse with one another and with their friends. When he made a commitment to Christ three years ago and was baptized, Bob hoped his anger would go away. But it is still there, and it leaves a residue of guilt every time he expresses it in inappropriate ways.

Reflecting on the course of his life, Bob realized that his own father had behaved the same way. But Bob Sr. was quicker to express his anger in physical ways—with the back of a hand or a leather belt. "That was the old-school way," Bob tells himself. "At least I'm not like that." Still, Bob frequently confronts his children with verbal tirades. Up to this point, they have always backed down in the face of this intimidating behavior. But Bob wonders if that will change someday—just as it changed for him in dealing with his own father.

The ways in which we apply power, especially in our families, are often rooted in the past. We parent our children in the ways we ourselves were raised. We react to family members based on past actions or conflicts. At the same time, we long for our children to remain as they were—young and dependent upon us. We crave stability, dependability.

It is counterintuitive, then, that the key to gaining and using power within our families is to relinquish the past. If our goal is to turn intention into action, then the past is truly dead, for we cannot perform any action there. But by identifying patterns, forgiving hurts, relinquishing grudges, and allowing traditions to be fluid, we free ourselves to act in the present. We have power.

The first step to gaining freedom from the past is to gain awareness of its hold on the present. Every family has patterns of behavior that it has developed over time. A pattern is any action that is seen as normative, an example to be copied. Sometimes these patterns are healthy for the family and the individuals who comprise it. At other times, family patterns are a source of dysfunction and destruction. Most families contain a mixture of patterns, both positive and negative.

Patterns are powerful. When we function according to an established family pattern, it feels natural and requires little effort. Yet when we attempt to break out of a pattern or establish a new one, it requires great energy to turn that intention into action. In most families, those who are most involved in creating the existing pattern are the least likely to see the need for change. Or they may realize that change needs to happen but be the last to fully embrace it. For instance, a parent who was raised in a strict home may react by becoming a parent who exercises very little discipline with his or her children. Similar to remodeling a house, altering the patterns of behavior within a family always exposes hidden problems. And like remodeling, it can end up costing twice as much and taking twice as long as expected.

While different families exhibit different patterns, most have some patterns in common. Typically, families contain three types of patterns: generational, relational, and developmental. To be wise stewards of power within our families, we must learn to assess these patterns and discover the power to make changes in them.

Generational Patterns

When conducting premarital counseling, I invite couples to focus on the phrase "two becoming one." When I ask what they think this means, they invariably say something about two individuals becoming one in marriage. That is the primary meaning, of course. But there is a secondary reality that often sneaks up on a couple. For in marriage, it is not only two personalities that are joined, but two people with unique family histories that must somehow merge into one family.

87

No man or woman enters marriage with a clean slate. We all come with certain expectations—normative examples, or patterns—of how a family should function. Sometimes we are aware of our presuppositions, and sometimes they operate subconsciously. In some cases, there is a good match between the family patterns of the bride and the groom; they have common assumptions about marriage, parenting, money, time usage, faith, and so on. Most of the time, however, there is a mismatch in expectations. That mismatch creates conflict in various areas, more positively described as opportunities for growth. In some cases, the patterns of both families of origin are healthy and beneficial, just different. More often one or both partners realize that they experienced unhealthy family patterns while growing up, and they don't want to pass them on to their children.

So there are generational patterns to cherish and build on, and there are generational patterns to break away from. The task of a married couple, then, is to determine at which points there should be continuity with the past and at which points to break the old patterns and begin new ones. There are at least two keys to identifying healthy patterns and building them into a family: awareness and forgiveness.

Power through Awareness

It is nearly impossible either to break away from or to build upon a pattern if you are unaware that it exists. That's why it is important for families to identify their normative examples of behavior and prayerfully consider whether they need to be embraced or rejected. Only when we are aware of a pattern can we take action upon it. There are three areas in which awareness is needed. The first is history.

History. All married people and parents in particular must develop an awareness of their personal histories. When I began a new relationship with a physician, he spent a good deal of time asking questions about my family history. He wanted to know if anyone closely related to me had suffered things like heart disease, diabetes, or alcoholism. My doctor knew that my history would create in me certain predispositions and that I would have to ensure I would not develop those illnesses. What is true of physical health is true of family health also. Families have unique predispositions that must be monitored and, if unhealthy, corrected.

In the area of developing awareness of family history, I have appreciated the *genogram* model developed by Peter Scazzero.[1] A genogram is a way of working back through your family tree to identify patterns that are prevalent in your personal history. As I have sought to develop this awareness for myself, I tried to discover how power tools such as money, sex, and anger were utilized both in my household of origin and the generations that preceded it.

It has been pointed out to me that I'm very disciplined when it comes to money and very wary of making unnecessary expenditures. Normally, this character trait is a strength. But the overextending of a strength can produce a weakness, and there have been times when the labels *cheapskate* or *tightwad* might well have been applied to me! As I researched my family history, I discovered that my parents also were cautious about personal expenditures, tending to be savers more than spenders. My mom's parents, too, were that way. As a young married couple, they had lost everything during the Great Depression.

It is probably true that my grandparents' experience influences the way I handle money, even though economic times are different and I have many more financial resources available to me. This attitude toward money is a generational pattern that is part of my personal history. There are many generational patterns, both positive and negative. Positively, parents and grandparents who spend their later years serving rather than pursuing leisure help generate a serving spirit in subsequent generations. Also, parents who create a family atmosphere in which feelings may be openly expressed can prevent children from feeling that they must bottle up their emotions. Negatively, patterns of sexual immorality, divorce, alcoholism, obesity, or criticism can be carried down through generations.

Tendencies. A second need for awareness is in the area of personal tendencies. Discovering how God has wired us emotionally, intellectually, and behaviorally is an endless adventure. His ability to create billions of human beings, each one unique, is beyond our comprehension. The philosopher's advice to "know thyself" is important for gaining awareness of the generational patterns at work in our lives. Yet the process of self-discovery shouldn't lead to self-absorption. It should produce a greater capacity to "love God with all your heart, soul, mind and strength" and to "love your neighbor as yourself" (Mark 12:30–31). Personal tendencies often develop into patterns, and those patterns can either inhibit or enhance our ability to exercise power.

Years ago I completed a behavioral survey that identified my style as expressive. That was supposed to mean that I enjoy interaction with people and am quick to enter into conversation. The survey also identified the backup style of expressive types, used when they are under pressure. The backup style? Verbal attacker. Self-examination has revealed that there is truth in both indications of the survey. So when I am feeling pressured at work, I must exercise care at home so I don't relieve that stress by verbally attacking my family. And when engaged in family conflicts, I am extremely cautious not to say things that I will later regret. It helps to be aware of our tendencies.

Every follower of Christ should have a sense of his or her spiritual gifts. I'm thankful for the many spiritual gifts surveys that are now so readily available. I've probably completed a dozen of them. These surveys aren't definitive indicators of our gifts, but they are useful for helping us reflect upon our experiences. In almost every survey I've taken, I've scored very high in the gift of leadership and very low in the gift of mercy. My own self-examination tells me that the results are accurate. So as a father, I must be aware that these tendencies may lead me to exercise too much control and show too little compassion as I relate to my children. While I don't tend toward the character quality of mercy, I am not excused from being merciful. Therefore I must discipline myself to develop mercy, and I am eager to do so because I realize that "blessed are the merciful, for they will be shown mercy" (Matt. 5:7).

Responses. A third area in which awareness is important is the area of responses. It is helpful for spouses and parents to know their most natural response to conflict. Of the many ways to respond to conflict, five are particularly ineffective yet common. As you consider them, it may be helpful to rank them from 1 to 5, with 1 being the response that you are most likely to use.

- Withdrawal
- Spiritualization
- Attack
- Blame
- Competition

The first response is withdrawal. Some respond to conflict by withdrawing from it while continuing to carry unresolved feelings because of it. Withdrawers find it easier to ignore the significance of a conflict, pretending it doesn't matter. While they may initially engage, they quickly surrender or exit before achieving resolution so that they can avoid confrontation.

The second response is spiritualization. Some people are quick to over-spiritualize a conflict, escaping into a let's-pray-about-it posture that is motivated more by a desire to manipulate the situation than to genuinely seek God. Spiritualizers may inappropriately apply Scripture or use a God-told-me approach to corner others in the conversation.

The third response is attack. Attackers target the person instead of the problem. They may attack immediately, or they may be retaliators who acquiesce at the time of the conflict but counterattack at a later time.

The fourth response is blame. Blamers fail to take responsibility for their part in the conflict, preferring to view it as the fault of someone or something else.

The fifth response is competition. Competitors desire to win at any cost. Rather than staying in the resolution process until a win-win solution can be identified, they work to get what they want and then view their selfish agenda as victory.

I have become aware that my tendency is to respond to conflict by withdrawal. That means when there is a conflict with my children, who are now young adults, I tend to avoid it. I hope that my wife Jan will address it so I don't have to or that given enough time, the problem will work itself out. This reaction has sometimes created an undue burden for my wife and robbed my children of an opportunity to really talk through what they were feeling and deciding. Armed with this awareness, I now seek to take the initiative in processing conflicts with our children. I've been blessed to discover the fears behind my withdrawal response rarely materialize. Instead, processing conflict has given greater opportunity for communication and intimacy.

Personal Patterns. In addition to history, tendencies, and conflict responses, there are a couple of other personal patterns that we must be aware of. One is energy level. I have a moderate level of energy, and I tend to have a good deal of energy for starting new things and less energy for sustaining them. So as a husband and father, I realize that I must budge my energy carefully to avoid being so drained by my demanding job that I have little energy left for my family. I also have to be cautious that I don't start things with my family that I fail to follow through on.

Another personal pattern has to do with strengths and weaknesses. Two resources are helpful in developing self-awareness in this area: *Now, Discover Your Strengths* and *Living Your Strengths*.[2] The thesis of both books, based on research by the Gallup organization, is that effectiveness increases when we concentrate on our strengths rather than on our weaknesses. Knowing one's strengths, therefore, is critical for the good stewardship of power.

I've discovered that one of my strengths is *focus*. A person with this strength can prioritize, act, follow through, and make the necessary corrections to stay on track with an initiative. That means that if I choose to set for myself the priority of meeting my wife's needs or of parenting my children, I will likely have the ability to turn those intentions into reality. However, if I don't set those priorities but instead focus my attention on my career or recreational activities, I can easily neglect my responsibility to my family. Understanding the power of that strength is critical for exercising power within my family.

I've mentioned several self-assessment tools including behavioral surveys, spiritual gifts tests, conflict style analysis, and the assessment of energy level and strengths. All have one thing in common: they help me understand my personal tendencies. These personal tendencies may reflect the patterns of previous generations in my family tree, and they may shape the generations to come. Having a greater level of self-awareness affords a greater opportunity to turn my intentions into action within my family. Without that awareness, I may fail to either capitalize on strengths or neutralize weaknesses, thereby allowing harmful patterns to continue operating in my family for years to come.

Power through Forgiveness

We have observed that power in any situation can be drawn from three sources. There is the internal capacity for power that exists within each person—we all have some God-given ability to turn intention into action. And there are two external sources of power: God's Spirit and evil. Within families, there is a temptation to draw power from the negative rather than the positive external source. That power comes in the form of hatred. Lewis Smedes puts it this way:

Hate does have a feel of power to it . . . To a person energized by hate, forgiving feels flaccid, sapless, impotent. We feel stronger when we nourish our contempt and plot to get even . . . Hate does generate a real energy. People who have been hurt and hate the villain who hurt them experience a surge of power inside.[3]

Sadly, some families are powered by hurt and hate for generations. But using hatred as a means to control a situation always backfires. As a young person I was taught something that I've seen proven over and over again: bitterness, revenge, and hatred bind the one who hates to the one who is hated. Some have described the bond of bitterness as equal in power to the bond of love. Those who hate keep their "enemy" constantly in mind. They think of the one they hate while awake and dream of him or her while asleep. Their enemy becomes their purpose for living. This preoccupation with the "enemy" only makes the one who hates more like the one hated. Far from gaining control of the person or situation, the one who hates eventually loses control of both.

That dynamic operates in family systems also. The daughter who hates her mother for screaming at her winds up screaming at her own children. The son who resents his father for being emotionally unavailable usually becomes distant from his own wife and children. Those who despise their parents will cringe at the comment "You're just like your father," or "You're just like your mother," but they ring true because the bond of bitterness causes them to relive the past rather than exercising the power to create a new pattern for the future.

Hatred can be a motivating force, at least initially. But over time, the energy to hate dies down. Eventually, hatred turns in on its creator, and the lack of forgiveness both saps the individual's soul and drains life and love from the family.

Forgiveness is what provides the energy to move forward. Forgiveness enables us to shake off the self-righteous deception of hatred and be honest about our shortcomings and the pain we've caused others. Forgiveness enables us to be hopeful that the future can be different from the past. Also, the ability to forgive is a prerequisite for initiating a confrontation or intervention in a family that is unhealthy. The reason many families live a lie rather than living in love is that family members lack the power to forgive. At some level they recognize that, and duplicity serves as a substitute for the integrity needed to deal honestly and lovingly with conflict.

When my oldest sons were young, I was preoccupied with the demands of ministry. It wasn't the unrealistic expectations of others but my own unreasonably high standards that drove me. I gave nearly all of my energy to pastoral work while my family received my emotional leftovers. I've had to ask each of my sons to forgive me for that, and I've demonstrated the fruit of repentance by placing a higher priority on my relationship with them and by being more available to them. Their forgiveness has freed them both from resentment in the present and the tendency to repeat this pattern of generational sin in the future. By seeking and receiving their forgiveness, I have been freed to pursue a future that is different from the past. Lewis Smedes observes, "Over the long run, love's power to forgive is stronger than hate's power to get even. I admit that hate gives temporary power for surviving today's brutality and it has a short-term power to move us into tough action for tomorrow. But hate lacks staying power to create a fairer future beyond revenge."[4]

My friend Jen Abbas writes from the perspective of an adult child of divorced parents. She speaks compellingly of the power of forgiveness in the process of making peace.

Making peace doesn't mean that we like the impact of the divorce or that we condone or accept it as good. It does mean that we acknowledge it, grieve it, and choose our response to it. We make peace with our pasts when we decide not to react to the present based on past experiences and hurts, but rather choose to respond in ways that enhance the futures we desire . . . Making peace in our relationships does not mean we'll live in perpetual bliss. It does mean we

choose to forgive and accept forgiveness, release resentment, and commit to the continuation of the relationship—
in whatever form it may need to take—rather than walk
away from a burned bridge.[5]

That bridge unburned may well span the gulf to a brighter future
and a healthier family for generations to come. I've discovered some
people need an invitation to forgive. It is as if they must be given permission to forgive or reassured that they have the power to do so. They
may have thought for years, "I can't forgive," or "I could never forgive
them for what they did." God's Word assures us that we do have the
power to forgive. That forgiveness may begin within the safety of dia-
logue with a trusted, mature Christian friend, pastor, or counselor. Wise
counsel often brings a clear focus, which is essential to forgiveness.

Looking Up
Focus on What Christ
Has Done *for* You

Looking Back
At What Was Done
to You

Looking Ahead
Focus on What Christ Can
Do *through* You

Bitterness develops when we consistently look back at what has been done *to* us. Forgiveness begins when we focus on what Christ has done *for* us. We can forgive in the same spirit and power in which Christ forgave us (Col. 3:13). We can move forward in a spirit of forgiveness as we focus on what Christ can do *through* us, taking what others may have meant for evil and realizing that God can bring good from it (Gen. 50:20). The power to forgive is expressed in the one-way act of releasing a person from our judgment and into God's justice. Reconciliation can come only if the person forgiven chooses to respond with honesty and humility. But even without reconciliation, those who forgive discover a brighter future because their hearts are clear.

Relational Patterns

A second set of powerful patterns in family life concerns the priority of relationships within the family system. Relationships among family members are reprioritized when a couple commits to marriage. This is a biblical reprioritization: "For this reason a man will leave his father and mother and be united to his wife . . ." (Gen. 2:24). Before marriage, the relationship with highest priority for both the man and the woman is their obligation to their parents—to honor their father and mother. This relationship is so important that God included it in his top-ten list of rules for being human, the Ten Commandments. But at the point of marriage, the relationship with parents becomes secondary to the relationship with the spouse and, eventually, with one's own children.

To be married is to leave one's parents, meaning to change the priority of one's relationship to them. Even adults sometimes relish the role of "mama's boy" or "daddy's girl," but such relationships spell trouble for a marriage. Many problems are caused in marriages where one or both partners never truly left home. Although they have physically moved away from home, some married people remain emotionally rooted in their household of origin. There is a world of difference between meeting the legitimate needs of our parents (honoring them as God commanded) and seeking to have *our* needs met through them.

Jan and I have begun to experience the separation that takes place when a child leaves home, not only by moving away but by creating another family. We have learned to be sensitive to the fact that the highest priority for our children is no longer our home but their own. Their first allegiance now belongs not with us but with the spouse that God has entrusted to them.

The ideal relational pattern for a family is to love the right things in the right order. It is challenging enough to love the right things and reject wrongful desires that undermine the foundation of the home. To love those good things in the right order is even more demanding.

Priority Ripples

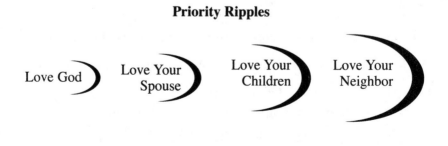

Love God   Love Your Spouse   Love Your Children   Love Your Neighbor

Priority One

The first priority for each of us is to love God. It is no coincidence that biblical teaching on marriage and the family is rooted in reverence for Christ (Eph. 5:21). When we love our spouse or children more than we love God, we've adopted the wrong priority. When we do so, we idolize our spouse or children, setting them in the place of God. This idolatry of the family occurs when family commitments take precedence over our love and devotion to God.

One of the more complicated challenges Jesus gives to those who wish to be His fully devoted followers is found in Luke 14:26: "If anyone comes to me and does not hate father and mother, wife and children, brothers and sisters—yes, even life itself—such a person cannot be my disciple." How can it be that we should hate our families in order to be Christ followers?

When most people hear the word *hate,* they think of intense dislike for something—a food, a person, a job, or an experience. But in the Bible, love and hate can refer to a choice between incompatible alternatives. When someone gives allegiance to another person or thing, he or she necessarily chooses to reject certain other people or things. This is why Jesus said, "No one can serve two masters. Either you will hate the one and love the other, or you will be devoted to the one and despise the other. You cannot serve both God and Money" (Matt. 6:24). So hatred in this context is a matter of devotion, not emotion. Therefore, even good things, and yes, even the best things like marriage and parenting, must not command our ultimate allegiance. That belongs to God alone. Jesus taught us that those who are unwilling to make their relationship with Him their ultimate priority could not be His disciples. Nothing should displace our allegiance to Him.

Priority Two

The second priority for a married person is to love one's spouse. Many couples lose their love for each other after children arrive. Willard Harley offers this warning:

> Most married couples think chemistry will keep them together because they're soul mates. Or they think that a commitment to stay married will guarantee their success. While both of these factors are important, millions of couples have discovered that they don't prevent divorce. When spouses neglect each other, they usually lose both chemistry and commitment.[6]

While the subject of this chapter is the stewardship of power within the family—not marriage per se—it is worth re-emphasizing that compatibility is nurtured through a continued commitment to serve one's spouse by meeting his or her needs. Being successful in marriage is not simply a matter of finding a perfect match. There is a strong connection between the primacy of marriage and the intimacy that is experienced in marriage.

The primacy of marriage is challenged by the demands of parenting. This is especially true of second marriages, where there is often a strong urge to place the needs of one's biological children ahead of one's spouse. Experienced parents realize that in any family, children will work to divide parents in order to get their way. Young children plead, "But Mommy said . . ." when they do not like what Daddy tells them. In the teenage years, such power plays become more intense.

One of our children went through a time of rebellion that was difficult for our entire family. In the midst of that difficulty, we talked with his youth pastor, seeking counsel on how to best manage this agonizing season of parenting. One bit of advice rings clear in my thinking nearly a decade later: "Whatever you do, don't let this child's behavior divide you. Keep your marriage strong so that your teen will have a loving home to return to later." That is sound advice. Thankfully, our child has now grown into a godly young adult. Jan and I are thankful that we did not allow the stress of parenting during that tumultuous time to alter the priority of relationships in our home. Some couples who experience difficulties within their family choose to withdraw from one another and pour all of their love and attention into their children. That is a tragic mistake. The best gift parents can give their children is to model a loving marriage for them. Children feel most loved not when parents lavish attention on them but when they receive the overflow of their parents' love for each other.

Priority Three

The third priority for those exercising good stewardship of power within the home is to love their children. In a very real sense, we are stewards of our children. They don't belong to us, ultimately, but to God, who has entrusted them to us during their most formative and

vulnerable years. As human parents, we raise our children for a relationship with their eternal Parent—their Heavenly Father. God's plan
is that our children should learn about His love through our love.

That's one of the reasons that dads are given this command: "Fathers,
do not embitter your children, or they will become discouraged" (Col.
3:21). Our love as fathers for our children will shape their relationship
both with God and with us. Many people have been so embittered by their
fathers that they must be re-taught the relationship between father and
child before they can think about God as a father figure.

Placing love for children as the third priority in the family may
leave the false impression that children are a low priority. But there
are so many things that are lower priority than our children. Sadly,
there are parents who love their pets more than they love their own
children. After all, pets, unlike children, are a source of unconditional
adoration. To love children unselfishly can be challenging. And there
are parents who love their careers more than they love their kids.
Perhaps that's because employees more often do what they're told
and clean up after themselves.

Some parents place their love for money ahead of their love for
their children. Over the years I've had several opportunities to
become acquainted with wealthy people. In many of their families,
wealth was used as a means to further God's kingdom and provide
opportunity for family members. In these families, the parents have
succeeded in keeping love for their children in the appropriate place
of importance. I have observed other families that were dysfunctional
even without wealth. Adding money to their situation was like throw-

ing gasoline on a fire. Little issues became big ones as money was used as a power tool within the family. In most cases, parents used money to control the behavior of their children. If they did what the parents wanted, money was either promised or released to them. If the children didn't "play by the rules," resources were withheld. I know of once case in which a daughter was prevented from asking tough ethical questions about the family business due to the threat of lost income. In another case, a daughter who was a caregiver to her parent was kept in constant subservience by the threat of being disinherited.

It is perfectly acceptable to use money as one means of reward or punishment for minor children. For example, it may be useful to withhold a child's allowance as a means of discipline or give him a special gift as an act of affirmation. That fits the rules-and-reward level of development that we'll explore in the coming pages. But to use money as a tool for manipulating adults hamstrings the development of a deeper and healthier relationship. Jesus himself said that it is impossible to love both God and money (Matt. 6:24). It may also be true that you can't love both family and money!

The use of money as a means of power creates tremendous competition among family members. Almost every conversation is somehow related to money, and siblings may war for years, even dragging the matter into the courts, in order to get their "fair share" of the family's wealth. The impact of the misuse of money as a means of control within a family is felt for generations.

It has been rightly said that money exercises immense power over everyone, but especially over those who have it.[7] We are intended to love family members and to use things. When parents instead love things and use their children, it leaves a wound in the soul. Children have a basic need to sense that their parents love them and to see that love demonstrated in two very visible places—in their finances and in their schedules.

Developmental Patterns

The third type of pattern that affects our ability to turn intention into action within our families is developmental. Our understanding of the various stages of a child's development has been greatly enhanced by secular researchers like Lawrence Kohlberg and by Christian specialists such as Ted Ward. One of the most important developmental dimensions for a child is how he or she relates to authority, especially moral authority. This marks the beginnings of a child's own stewardship of power. Kohlberg identifies three levels that account for virtually all moral judgment.[8]

Level one is preconventional judgment, which focuses on me and my concerns. "Good" is what serves my purposes or makes me feel good. "Bad" or "wrong" is what hurts me or my interests. So a person, usually a young child, in this phase of moral judgment is affected most by the use of reward or punishment.

Level two is conventional judgment, which focuses on others. In this stage, moral judgments take into account factors beyond the self. In the early stages of this level, the determination of right and wrong is based on what pleases or displeases the people who are important to me. In the later stages of this level, rules and regulations provide clear guidance as to what is right and wrong. For the Christians, it's at this level that the WWJD question becomes a concern: What would Jesus do?

Level three is postconventional judgment, which focuses on principles. Moral judgments are made based on principles that provide a foundation for the behavior I value in myself and others.

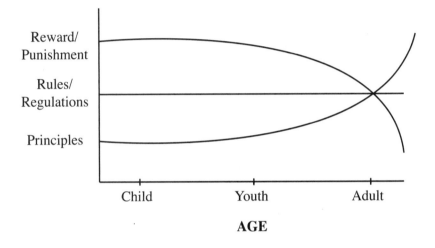

AGE

Kohlberg's research showed that most people start at the first level and pass through level two to level three in a predictable sequence. Not everyone progresses through the levels, however. Some people remain in the first or second levels of moral decision making, basing their judgments of right and wrong on their most immediate needs or on the desire to please others. Kohlberg also found that people best understand moral messages that are tuned in to their level.

As Christians, we can interpret our journey to spiritual maturity in light of these levels. God rewards and punishes, but He also seeks to write His laws in our hearts (see 2 Cor. 3:3) and to have a valued relationship with us as His children. God wants us to believe what we believe and do what we do based not on external rules only, but also on internalized principles that flow from our relationship with Him. God wants us to progress to the most mature level of moral judgment as we respond to His authority.

A challenge for parents is to recognize that their stewardship of power within their families must change as their children develop. Early on, it is appropriate for children to receive reward or punishment for their behavior, so discipline is given in tangible forms. But as children begin to mature, they need clear rules within the context of good relationships to continue their moral development. Ultimately, we want them to act independent of parental authority. To do that, they must develop their own faith in Christ and the moral convictions that flow from it. God has many children but no grandchildren. No adult can get by on the second-hand faith received from parents. Each of us must finally relate to God on our own.

As we seek to be good stewards of power with our children, we must discern their level of moral judgment and exercise our authority in ways appropriate to that level. Our children are born in complete dependence upon us and must grow to independence. That means that as our children progress through the levels of moral development, we must gradually relinquish our control over them.

Parents must face the fundamental truth that they cannot retain previous levels of control over their children as they pass from one stage of development to another. But there is a positive side to this surrender of authority. As parents, we gain even more power within our families by surrendering the control we already have—or think we have. This principle is rooted in the biblical teachings of Jesus, who showed us that the way to gain is to surrender and that the way to live is to die.

The surrender of control by a parent involves both the child's behavior and the underlying beliefs that support it. As children progress through developmental levels, and especially as they reach level three, parents must increasingly affirm the beliefs that support them in enabling their children rather than tightly controlling them. Parents must come to believe statements such as these:

- A change scenario exists that will meet all of our needs as a family.
- It is desirable to search for a change that meets all of our needs.
- Everyone and every viewpoint is of worthy of consideration in the decision-making process.
- The views of other family members are legitimate statements of their positions.
- Differences of opinion can be helpful.
- Other members of the family are trustworthy.

It is true that during times of rebellion children may not hold legitimate viewpoints or be trustworthy. Yet many parents embitter their children by refusing to let them grow up. These parents exercise power and maintain control in ways that are more appropriate to previous developmental stages.

A child's transition to independence can be agonizing for parents, especially if the child is making poor choices. Recently my wife and I visited with a couple at a local coffee shop. This couple knew that we had helped our three children navigate the transition to adulthood and that those experiences had created more than a little rough water—maybe even a few tsunamis! This couple was enduring a difficult season with one of their teens. They had invested themselves in creating a loving relationship with their teen. They had provided appropriate levels of moral authority—progressing from rewards and punishments to rules and relationships, and finally to instilling principles. Their teen was still making poor choices, and they were rightfully concerned that these choices could bring consequences that would endure for years to come. This is every parent's fear. Yet as Ted Ward reminds us, the harsh truth about parental power is that while "parents set patterns or models for their children's moral judgments, each child builds his or her own structure of moral judgment. Parents can't pass it down. The parents' example does not produce moral conscience in the child."[9]

It helps me to think of my parental power in my relationship to my children in this way:

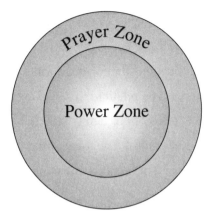

As a parent, there are certain aspects of my children's lives that I am able to control. There are many other things in their lives that are beyond the circle of my power but within the circle of God's power. I know that only the power of prayer will make a difference in those things. Concerning things outside my power zone, I have two choices: worry or pray, and the Bible commands me not to worry. When I worry, I hang on to the things that are beyond my power to control. When I pray, I release them to God. More accurately, I admit to God that I am powerless over them and ask for His intervention.

As parents we must provide leadership through concrete guidelines and wise counsel. We must exercise compassionate but firm discipline as we train our children for higher levels of moral judgment and independence. We must relinquish control while retaining a relationship in which we are both vulnerable and available. And we must do all we can to connect our children with the ultimate authority in their lives and ours, Jesus Christ.

Within our families, change is not merely inevitable, but desirable and necessary. Fear leads us to cling to the past—unhealthy patterns of thought and action, improper priorities for our allegiance, former levels of authority in relationships. As we become more aware of ourselves and the needs of our family members, we are enabled to relinquish the sense of control that comes from clinging to the past, and we are enabled to turn our best intentions for the present and future into reality. We have power.

For Further Thought

1. What does the Bible mean when it says that in marriage "two become one"?

2. List some of the generational patterns that operate in your life and in your spouse's. Which patterns do you have in common? What are the greatest differences?

3. How were the power tools of sex and money used in your family of origin?

4. Which conflict resolution response best describes your reaction to conflict? Which ones did your parents use?

5. The author makes the assertion that love and hatred have nearly equal power in the life of a person. Do you agree?

6. Which do you think requires more power, hatred or forgiveness? Which is more empowering?

7. The author uses the term *idolatry of family* to describe placing a higher priority on family than on God. Do you think the term is too strong?

8. Describe the relationship between primacy and intimacy in a marriage.

9. Describe the effect upon children when parents place a higher value on their marriage than on meeting their children's needs. Is this healthy or unhealthy, in your opinion?

10. Name some instances of money being used as a power tool to exercise control within a family.

11. At what level of moral development do you see your children? What signs have you seen, if any, that they may be ready to change levels?

12. Do you believe that parents are responsible for the choices their children make? Explain your answer.

The Power to Contribute

Arena of Power: Workplace

Source of Power: Stewardship

Power Principle: I do not own the power to rule; it is given to me as a trust.

Jerry joined a small group of men from his church who had made a six-week commitment to explore their career paths. They met at a coffee house each Tuesday on their way to work. Most of those present were interested in building upon the "success" they had already experienced in order to achieve greater levels of "significance" in the future. Jerry listened intently as others shared about their careers—some in corporations, some in smaller family-owned businesses, and others in companies they had created themselves.

When it was Jerry's turn to share, he was unsure if he could tell his story to the other men. But he opened his mouth, and the words began to flow. Jerry recounted that he had spent twenty years climbing the corporate ladder at a telecommunications firm. He had made great sacrifices of time, including a great deal of travel. His life had revolved around his work, and he admitted that he really hadn't had time for God. But in a single day, that had all ended. Fighting to control his emotions, Jerry told how he had gone from a position of power and prestige to unemployment after the buyout of his company by a major corporation. He had gone from enjoying a high level of purchasing power due to his substantial income to having no income and very little economic power. "Twenty years," Jerry repeated. "And it was over in a single day."

That loss of power prompted a search. Jerry began to ask questions about ultimate meaning. What is really important in life? Why go to work? Is it possible to do something that both brings success in the world's eyes and also seems significant from God's perspective? Jerry was determined to find out.

Company presidents have the power to affect the lives of thousands of people. Government leaders affect the lives of millions. In both settings, leaders have a measure of control over the lives of others. They have the power to rule. Rulers often believe that this power is theirs by right. Employees are promoted based on their good performance. Company leaders are appointed by a board. Politicians are elected by the people. Often, those in power see their authority as earned and, therefore, as deserved. Yet authority is never earned; it is always given. Ultimately, all authority comes from God, who gave dominion over the world to human beings. We exercise power in trust from God, regardless of the means by which it is acquired. Stockholders give to a CEO the authority to operate a company.

Executives give authority to their managers. Voters give authority to elected officials. In all cases, the authority is given by others, who themselves hold it in trust.

The key to exercising power, then, is to manage that trust wisely. When we believe that we have a right to power, we are likely to be corrupted by it. When we humbly recognize that the authority we hold is a gift to be wisely used, we use power well.

The Dynamics of Power in Leadership

One of my mentors has provided long-term leadership in his company. For decades he has steadily climbed the corporate ladder, not because he intentionally sought power but because he faithfully and humbly carried out his assignments. As he exercised good stewardship of the power entrusted to him, he was promoted to increased levels of authority. He is a living example of the servant in Jesus' story to whom the master said, "You have been faithful with a few things; I will put you in charge of many things" (Matt. 25:21). Jim Collins, author of *Good to Great,* might label my friend a Level 5 Leader because he masterfully combines the personal humility and professional will.

Occupying the Seat of Power

One day Bob and I were having breakfast, and he casually used the term *seat of power* during our conversation. I've learned that nuggets of prized wisdom often come in the form of casual comments from learned people, so I pressed him to define the term. It

117

m he'd coined to apply to people who have been given a significant measure of authority. Bob related that over the years he has observed many people who were changed as they occupied the seat of power. Some had come to believe that they owned it. Convinced both that they deserved the seat of power and that no one could fill it quite like they could, these power embezzlers became prideful.

From that point, according to Bob, events would follow a predictable trajectory. The pride generated by power tended to destroy teamwork and cause the organization to be celebrity centered rather than results oriented. Believing the lie that "it's all about me," these misguided leaders would consistently act in ways intended to protect their place of power. In time, they became convinced that the power emanated from them rather than that it was given to them. Generally, a personal or business failure would ensue.

That abuse of power is apt to creep up on any leader who sees power as a personal right rather than a privilege given by virtue of position. Most do not begin with the intention to abuse power; they are drawn into its darker side by the sin of pride.

People are affected not only by occupying the seat of power but also by leaving it. Sometimes that is the moment when it dawns on them that power never belonged to them and must be left behind. They have seen that borrowed power so much as a part of their identity that they don't know who they are when not in the power seat. It is challenging both to use power rightly and to leave it well. As my conversation with Bob continued, he mused that perhaps some corporate seats of power should have term limits as the United States presidency does. When one person spends too much time in the seat of power in any organization, it tends to move both the leader and the group away from democracy and toward dictatorship.

Stewarding the Responsibility of Power

As we lingered over a second cup of coffee, Bob sketched the profile of some other leaders he's observed: those who have learned to sit lightly in the seat of power. He noted that they have some things in common. One is the recognition that they occupy the seat of power only temporarily. In most cases, someone else occupied that seat before them and someone else will sit in it when they are gone. Good stewards of power refuse to believe the lie that power belongs to them.

Second, good stewards of power do not allow others to confuse their power with their personhood. Those around a power-full leader often try to place that leader on a pedestal because they see him or her only in terms of power and not as a real person. That mistake is often made with pastors, politicians, physicians, and other professionals. When leaders allow the seat of power to become a pedestal, they make themselves vulnerable to duplicity and deception. Often they must work intentionally at breaking down the pedestal by revealing to others that they live real, even ordinary, lives. Good stewards of power are fully aware that while they sit in the seat of power at work, they sit in a pew at church and in a recliner at home. They recognize that holding power is only one aspect of their lives. That balanced perspective repels the delusion that has overtaken many who have occupied the power seat.

Third, good stewards of power work to prevent their control of authority to degrade into ownership. These contrasts remind us of the difference.

Stewardship	Ownership
Is Team Driven	Is Me Centered
Shares the Spotlight	Casts Others in the Shadows
Builds a Broad Base of Relationships	Has Only Work-Related Relationships
Produces a Balanced Life	Causes Life to Revolve around Work
Affirms and Promotes Others	Suppresses or Sabotages Others

Fourth, those who occupy the power seat well also recognize the one-two punch that can deliver a knockout to any leader: the seduction of money added to the seduction of power. Those who do well as stewards of power usually do well with the stewardship of money also.

Bob's stewardship of power has not only helped him to live well but also has helped his company to prosper. Nearing the sunset of his career, Bob is still willing to take risks that benefit those he leads. The company that he directs was recently acquired by another, and his leadership skills has been recognized within the parent company. Bob is now engaged in an effort to transform the larger company's culture. In another casual comment delivered as we left the restaurant, Bob said, "If you want to change a culture, pack a lunch." It was his way of noting that attempting so great a task is both difficult and risky. Because he sits lightly in the power seat, Bob can afford to take those risks. H⌣ knows that if he is sent packing and is no longer able to occupy the seat of power, he will continue to live a successful and rewarding life.

The Dynamics of Power in the Workplace

If power is the capacity to turn intention into reality, then leaders must have power; without it, they cannot lead. That the stewardship of power involves the management of energy is not a recent discovery. As we learned earlier, the New Testament uses the Greek word *energma* to describe power that is applied to bring about a result. That Greek term is the root of our word *energy*.

All of us bring energy to our workplaces whether we occupy a seat of power or not. We energize our work environments with either positive or negative energy. Social scientist Bertrand Russell observed, "The fundamental concept in social science is power, in the same sense in which energy is the fundamental concept in physics"[1] So whether we work on the production floor of a factory, in an office cubicle, at a customer service call center, or travel the country as a sales representative, we all exercise power and are all impacted by it. How does that power operate?

Ingredients of Power

The dynamics of power in all organizations make use of the ingredients of power mentioned in the introduction to this book: inspiration, intelligence, influence, and investment. These ingredients are perhaps more critical for developing the capacity to turn intention into action in the workplace than in any other arena of life.

Inspiration. For a Christian, the use of power always begins with inspiration. I believe God's Spirit prompts our intentions and empowers our actions in the workplace just as He does at church. To effectively convert our intentions into action, we must be sure that we are properly motivated—not self-motivated. We must begin each day by asking God for wisdom in solving problems, relating to coworkers, and seeing new opportunities to improve the companies that employ us.

Intelligence. We often have a well-developed awareness of ourselves and our families. We need that awareness in order to effectively relate to others. That is as true at work as in other arenas. We must be students of our jobs, eager to learn how we can do them to the best of our abilities. That involves gathering information, whether it be data, technical knowledge, political intelligence, or expertise. Often, the application of power is needed to solve workplace problems. Defining the problem is the first step, and that requires the acquisition and application of information to shape a feasible, focused solution. Gathering intelligence begins with asking the question, "What do I need to know?" I dream of the day when Christians will be generally known as the most devoted lifelong learners in their workplaces.

Influence. Power in the workplace may be positional, being attached to a certain position on the company's organizational chart. Workplace power may also be derived from a less formal source— influence. Sometimes our influence is limited by factors beyond our control. More often, influence is limited by a lack of energy devoted to acquiring it. When we are respected by others, we have power. The development of influence requires networking with others, and it involves seeking approval for our intentions from those who are more influential than we are. The time taken to invest in relationships with others can produce openness to our ideas. Sometimes a coalition is needed in order to gain enough support for an idea. That requires the development of a network of backers who agree to support and perhaps provide resources for implementing change. Developing influence means asking the question "Who do I need to connect with?"

Investment. Investment in the workplace is not a matter for stock traders only. Every person who hopes to turn intention into action in the arena of work must have the resources required to do so. Those resources could include time, money, materials, space, technology, or any other needed item. Sadly, many workers give up before adequate resources can be gathered and emotionally exit from the challenge of creating change—even if they don't physically exit by resigning from the job. Gathering the resources to invest in change can be time consuming. It requires patience. Preparing to invest means asking the question "Where can I go for additional resources?"

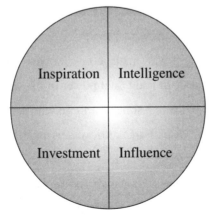

Capital Management

Many people complain about problems in the workplace but feel powerless to effect change. It is true, as Rosabeth Moss Kanter has pointed out, that much of the energy needed to initiate change is consumed in gathering the required resources: "Innovations require a search for additional supplies, for additional 'capital,' elsewhere in the organization. Thus, a great deal of the innovation process consists of a search for power."[2]

The stewardship of power in our workplaces requires us to search for and wisely manage additional capital in the form of power. What distinguishes the Christian worker is that this search for power is never self-focused. The power gained is not to be used for personal benefit but for the benefit of those we serve. In the words of Jesus, "Whoever wants to become great among you must be your servant, and whoever wants to be first must be your slave—just as the Son of Man did not come to be served, but to serve" (Matt. 20:26–28). Yet when our focus is to serve others, it is quite often the case that we are blessed as well. The right attitude for seeking power in the workplace includes three primary characteristics.

Humility. For those who manage or supervise the work of others, employees are a source of additional power in the workplace. We seek to influence and gain the investment of those who are under our authority. It's vital that we display the spirit of servanthood as we deal with those who may be under us, who look to us for leadership and supervision. Richard Foster states, "On the job, power is to be used to facilitate competence, not promote feelings of inadequacy. The business world is one place in which a Christian witness to creative power is desperately needed. Subordinates often feel helpless and manipulated, but it does not need to be this way."[3] Good stewards of power are humble.

Empowerment. A second distinguishing characteristic of Christians in the workplace is that they empower those who work for them. Besides being the Christlike thing to do, empowering others is simply good for an organization. Rosabeth Kanter puts it this way: "The degree to which the opportunity to use power effectively is granted to or withheld from individuals is one operative difference between those companies which stagnate and those which innovate."[4] We gain power not to enrich ourselves by creating a power base, but in order to share it appropriately with others. A mentor of mine started a furniture design company when he was in his fifties. This man is a wonderful combination of artist and leader, which is beneficial not only for product development but also for people development. He has surrounded himself with staff members more than twenty years his junior. When I meet with him, I can sense his passion as he talks about the way the younger people on his leadership team are developing. His approach is leading to success in the marketplace today and to a bright and energetic future as these young leaders emerge.

Encouragement. We normally think of power in the workplace as being applied downward to those who are beneath us organizationally, or perhaps horizontally to our peers. But power can also be applied upward to those who are in leadership over us. Many workers put a great deal of effort into leading down but little or no effort in leading up. Some employees wrongly believe that they have no power in an organization because have no direct reports—that is, they don't super-vise the work of anyone else. In reality, they may have significant power that does not appear on the organizational chart. Foster calls this the power of encouragement:

> It may be hard for us to believe, but it is lonely at the top. Executives find that genuine friendships are hard to come by, because people fear their power. And those who do not fear it often are hoping to use it. Employees who follow the way of Christ will reach out to their employers . . . This, too, is a ministry of power.[5]

Negatively, we sometimes see this power applied in the manipulation of leaders by their employees. That can take the form of flattery or passive-aggressive behavior. Christian employees can and should use the power of encouragement for positive ends. Actions such as suggesting improvements, taking initiative, and praising the good decisions of managers will both empower those in leadership and will shift power capital to the employee.

Whether we are leading up, down, or laterally, the hardest person to lead is often ourselves. Being a good steward of power in the work-place demands that we be good stewards of ourselves. Perhaps that is why the art of "self-leadership" has become such a hot topic among business leaders. Managing power in the workplace begins with self-discipline. Fortunately, we have some biblical models for managing both self and others well.

A Model of Power: Daniel

The personal character traits that lends themselves to the good stewardship of power are displayed in the lives of two great biblical leaders. The first is Daniel, who rose to leadership in a large government bureaucracy, one that operated on values that were often at odds with his personal faith. His story offers insights that provide a starting point for the self-assessment of our own stewardship of power in the workplace.

My good friend Bill has been very successful in building brokerage offices in my home city, Grand Rapids, Michigan. Bill is also a student of the Word, and he seeks daily to integrate his faith with his work. One day he shared with me his admiration for Daniel. He remarked about Daniel's resiliency and his capacity to rise to the top in three different administrations—a truly noteworthy accomplishment.

Bill is not the first business leader I have known who drew inspiration from the life of Daniel. This Old Testament hero offers many lessons on the stewardship of power in the workplace. Daniel was one of the most powerful people of his day. Like many believers today, he faced the challenge of honoring God in an environment where his faith was not fully appreciated. Daniel's career was in government service. He was a city manager for one of the greatest cities in the world. That city, Babylon, would find its equivalent today in cities such as New York, London, or Tokyo. Daniel did not come to live in Babylon by choice, nor was his position of power something he envisioned for himself. His emigration from ancient Israel to Babylon was forced. Yet within a short time after he arrived, Daniel was on a career path that would lead him to great power.

What allowed Daniel to rise to a position of such great influence while working in a career that he did not choose and in an environment hostile to his faith? Undoubtedly, he was blessed with supernatural gifts from God that were unique to him—what we might call his unique genius. In that sense, not everyone can be a Daniel. Yet he also demonstrated some characteristics that any one of us can incorporate into our lives. Daniel displayed credibility, integrity, and security in his use of power in the workplace—and so can we.

Credibility

Daniel, along with his believing coworkers, did outstanding work, and that gave them tremendous credibility with their superiors. Soon after his arrival in Babylon, Daniel was drafted into a management training program. Our introduction to this young man comes as he is respectfully asking his supervisor for permission to follow his faith convictions, promising that this will not adversely affect his job performance. When Daniel is given permission to test this assertion by conducting a pilot project, the results prove that abiding by his convictions strengthened both his physical body and his job performance (Dan. 1:8–17). Relating to coworkers in a respectful way, especially concerning matters of faith, always increases our credibility and strengthens the companies we work in.

Daniel exhibits another discipline that appears to have been rare in his workplace and is certainly uncommon today. He pursued excellence. Daniel focused his attention on doing his job well while avoiding forays into organizational politics. His performance standard was not determined by *comparison* to others but by *submission* to God.

Throughout the book of Daniel, we read that he distinguished himself in his work, which gave him favor with his superiors and made him the envy of his coworkers. Eventually, he was appointed as one of the top three administrators in the entire nation. This leadership team of three had 120 direct reports, who were responsible for the management of the empire. Now that's an impressive span of control!

Among these top three leaders, Daniel soon distinguished himself as the best (Dan. 6:3). Predictably, the others became jealous and began to scheme against Daniel. Because they could find nothing about his job performance that would discredit him, they use Daniel's faith against him. Daniel was known as a man of prayer. Realizing that he would not deviate from his practice of prayer, Daniel's enemies flattered the king's ego and induced him to pass a law against praying to anyone or anything other than himself. Daniel disobeyed that unjust law and prayed to God, as was his habit. You probably know the rest of the story—although he realized that Daniel had been the victim of a plot, the king was compelled to enforce his own law. He ordered that Daniel be thrown into the lions' den, where God miraculously protected him overnight. The next day, the outraged emperor fed Daniel's accusers to those same lions.

I am especially impressed by Daniel's remark, delivered while still in the den of lions. When the king went to see if Daniel had been devoured, Daniel greeted him with these words: "O king, live forever!" (Dan. 6:21). I suspect that most of us would have responded quite differently. Yet we have no evidence in this situation or at any other time that Daniel entertained thoughts of revenge or even engaged in the petty politics that plague so many organizations. He certainly would have been aware of how others despised him because of his work performance and faith, but Daniel kept the focus on doing his job and on honoring his ultimate boss—the God to whom he prayed three times each day.

Daniels model of credibility offers a gauge for assessing ourselves. On a scale from 0 to 5, with 0 being never and 5 being always, rate your credibility in the workplace based on the following list of behaviors.

_____ I present requests to my superiors in a respectful manner.

_____ I hold faith convictions that strengthen the culture of my organization.

_____ I focus on meeting my responsibilities, not what others are doing.

_____ I avoid involvement in petty political disputes.

Exercising power in the workplace depends upon having credibility with our bosses, coworkers, and employees.

Integrity

Integrity is a second aspect of Daniel's character that enhanced his ability to wield power in the workplace. In Daniel's case, the fact that he followed his convictions unwaveringly nearly always led to some benefit both for his employer and for himself. It is a wonderful thing to be a person of integrity in an environment where that is appreciated, even celebrated. But what happens when the demands of your employment conflict with your personal convictions?

By *personal convictions,* I mean deeply held faith principles, not trivial opinions or preferences. Daniel's convictions were matters of genuine obedience to God. Some people, on the other hand, have "convictions" about nearly everything and tend to frame every action or decision as a spiritual matter. It's important for people of faith to distinguish between principle and preference. It's dangerous to spiritualize matters of personal preference and to elevate them to the status of convictions when they are really a matter of comfort. Within one week I had two conversations with people about their workplace demands. One expressed concern about having to work on Sundays, and she framed it as a matter of conviction. But as she gave her reasons for wanting Sundays off, I noticed that most of them revolved around the desire to enjoy leisure time with family rather than matters of faith. A couple of days later, another person expressed concern about having been told by his supervisor that he was not allowed to wear a t-shirt with a Christian message on it. As the story unfolded, I sensed that the employer's concern was not only about the message that the shirt displayed but also about the manner in which the employee was dressed. The apparel did not meet the level of professionalism desired by the employer.

But there are times when workplace conflict occurs over matters of principle. Daniel's decision to continue praying to God in spite of the law to the contrary is one example. Earlier in Daniel's story, he and his fellow Jewish immigrants—Shadrach, Meshach, and Abednego—faced a similar conflict when they were required to bow in reverence to an idol. To do so would have violated the clear instruction of Scripture—the second commandment. They refused to comply and faced the fiery furnace as a result. The three were loyal employees who had earned their boss's respect. They had carried out their responsibilities in a way that led to promotion and recognition. But the limit of their otherwise legitimate loyalty to their nonbelieving employer came when that employer called them to violate their conscience. Their primary loyalty to God rightly took precedence over their secondary loyalty to their employer. Here is what their superior told them:

> Is it true, Shadrach, Meshach and Abednego, that you do not serve my gods or worship the image of gold I have set up? Now . . . if you are ready to fall down and worship the image I made, very good. But if you do not worship it, you will be thrown immediately into a blazing furnace. Then what god will be able to rescue you from my hand? (Dan. 3:14–15).

The king called them to do something that both he and they knew would compromise their allegiance to God. In this case—as always, in matters of integrity—the king believed that their interest in self-preservation would outweigh their desire to obey God. He was wrong.

There may come a time when you are asked to do something that violates your core convictions. You may be asked to lie in order to enhance the reputation of your company or its brand image. You may be expected to engage in a business activity that is unethical or illegal. You may be pressured to be involved in promoting a product that you know is harmful to others. In each case, some aspect of self-preservation will be pitted against your desire to be obedient. This is a real test of the stewardship of power. None of us risk being thrown into a fiery furnace when we stand for our convictions. But we may pay a price—loss of income, failure to receive a raise or promotion, demotion, termination of employment. When faced with such a situation, it will be tempting to cast the unethical or immoral behavior in the most righteous of terms. We may deceive ourselves into believing that the most important thing is to maintain our position of power.

How did Daniel's three compatriots respond to their dilemma? They respectfully but firmly asserted that they would not violate the dictates of their conscience. While respectfully acknowledging the king's authority over their immediate future, they simultaneously made clear that their ultimate well-being was not in his hands but in God's. They submitted themselves in obedience to God, no matter what the future held (Dan. 3:16–18). That vertical focus—seeing God's power as primary in their lives and the king's power as secondary—was the source of their integrity. When I think my well-being ultimately depends on my employer, I may compromise my integrity out of loyalty to the company. When I am constantly aware that God is my ultimate boss and has final say in my career, I am empowered to act with complete integrity in the workplace.

It is important to respond to ethical dilemmas with the same spirit as did the three Jewish men—respectfully but firmly. Sometimes standing for convictions can create a spirit of self-righteousness or condescension toward others. When we stand for the right value with the wrong attitude, it deflects attention from the real moral issue at hand. It is possible to take a stand humbly and respectfully, yet firmly.

The integrity of Shadrach, Meshach, and Abednego offers another yardstick for self-assessment. Again, rate yourself from 0 to 5 based on the following statements.

_____ I am aware of the difference between my preferences and my principles.

_____ I am able to maintain a respectful attitude when feeling threatened by workplace circumstances.

_____ I am constantly aware that my primary loyalty is vertical (to God) and not horizontal (to my employer).

Those who have integrity tend to gain power in the workplace. Those who lack integrity generally lose power over the long run. Integrity is critical for the stewardship of power at work.

Security

A third quality displayed by Daniel that is important for the wise use of power in the workplace is security—that is, having knowledge of the ultimate source of his security. How easy it is to derive a sense of security from the wrong sources, things like job titles or retirement accounts. If our security is found in those work-related things, we will be powerless to maintain our credibility and act with integrity when we feel threatened or insecure.

Daniel and his coworkers made it clear that while they did their jobs to the best of their ability, their professional identity, their reputation, and their success were not the sources of their security. God was their ultimate employer and provider. Having that perspective allowed them to stand firm in faith and not succumb to fear.

Who or what ultimately provides for your family? You? Your employer? Your medical insurer? Your investment broker? We gratefully acknowledge the role of our employer as the immediate provider of income and benefits that contribute to our well-being. Yet if we do not see beyond that immediate source to the God who provides for all of our needs, we will most likely find ourselves asking, "If I don't do what the job requires, how will I make it financially?"

Instead, we should be asking questions like, "If I don't do what God requires, what will become of me?" Our security comes from our relationship to our Eternal Employer, not our earthly employer. It is God whom we need to satisfy. If we focus on doing that, our earthly employer will benefit as well because we will function at our highest level.

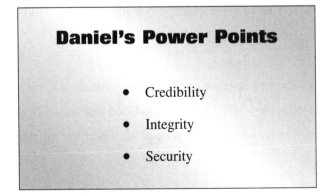

Daniel's Power Points

- Credibility
- Integrity
- Security

Sometimes the immediate and ultimate sources of security get tangled up in our minds. If your home entertainment center is like mine, behind the well-ordered façade there is a tangle of power cords and wires. When something goes wrong with the television or DVD player, the first challenge is to untangle that mass of cords to expose the problem. As the number of electronic devices in our home has increased, that can be a tremendous challenge! Sometimes the "power cords" of our credibility, integrity, and security get tangled up so that we are not sure if the power in our lives is coming from God or from our employer. It is critical to keep that relationship untangled. God is our ultimate source of security.

Rate your security level by responding to the statements below. Again, use the 0 to 5 scale.

_____ I am grateful for the compensation provided by my employer.

_____ I nearly always recognize that God is the ultimate provider of resources in my life.

_____ I find greater contentment in honoring God than in reviewing my financial accounts.

Those who feel insecure or who believe that their security is self-generated are unlikely to use power well. Good stewards of power in the workplace have a clear understanding of what is ultimately important.

A Model of Power: Paul

A second biblical leader provides an example of good stewardship of power in the workplace. The Apostle Paul was a small-business owner whose enterprise supported his ministry. In 1 Thessalonians 4:11–12, Paul gives practical advice for applying power through influence, especially in the lives of those who are outside of the community of faith. Paul was a tentmaker by trade, and he chose to use his ability to generate income to support his ministry. His job in the marketplace—making tents—provided enough resources that he did not have to depend on contributions from others to underwrite his mission endeavors. So this advice originates from a man who held a day job while passionately pursuing his ministry. Here's what he says:

> Make it your ambition to live a quiet life, to mind your own business and to work with your hands, just as we told you, so that your daily life may win the respect of outsiders and so that you will not be dependent on anybody.

We might easily miss some of the points made in this verse if we fail to understand the context in which it was written. Let's examine this statement more closely.

Humility

Paul's commands to "live a quiet life" and "work with your hands" might lead a person to believe that manual labor is the only acceptable form of Christian work. But there is a higher message. In the Greek culture of Paul's day, manual labor was thought to be degrading. So for a learned man like Paul to work with his hands—and to call others to do the same—was a sign of humility. Paul is saying something like this: Do your work with humility, and focus more on doing what is necessary than on your own status.

Those who are good stewards of power in the workplace are invariably known for their humility. In his best-selling book, *Good to Great,* Jim Collins identifies what he calls Level 5 Leaders.[6] These are individuals who have given sustained and superior leadership to the companies entrusted to them. These leaders exhibit a rare combination of personal humility and professional will. Their humility is demonstrated by an it's-not-about-me decision-making style, a willingness to give credit to others, and an aversion to seeking celebrity status. This humility is combined with a passion to lead their companies to success no matter what the obstacles may be. This professional will is akin to what the Bible calls perseverance. It is fascinating that Collins, analyzing the dynamics of the modern-day world of business, validates the leadership style that Paul exhibited nearly two thousand years ago. Contrary to what we might think, humility does not detract from a leader's power but enhances it.

Let's continue using the 0 to 5 scale for self-assessment. Rate yourself in the following areas, all connected with personal humility and its effect on influence in the workplace. Remember that 0 means never, and 5 means almost always.

_____ I am more concerned with doing what needs to be done than with being noticed for my achievements.

_____ I readily give others credit for their contribution.

_____ I make decisions based primarily on what is best for the company, not on what is best for me personally.

What do the results of this assessment say about your level of humility at work?

Personal Responsibility

Paul's advice couples personal humility with a strong sense of personal responsibility. This combination never fails to win the respect of others. Paul's command to Christians to mind their own business reminds us that we are not to be distracted in fulfilling our responsibilities. When we gossip, compare our work with that of others, or blame others when things don't go as planned, we are avoiding personal responsibility.

More than once, I've read the engaging little book _QBQ! The Question Behind the Question._ In it, author John Miller explains the need for practicing personal accountability at work and in other areas of life. As the title indicates, that involves asking questions of personal responsibility that underlie our desire to blame others, complain, or procrastinate. The Apostle Paul might call them MYOB questions— meaning _mind your own business_!

Paul's advice continues by naming the desired result of personal humility and responsibility—respect and independence. He says that when his readers display these twin attitudes in their work, they will "win the respect of outsiders" and "will not be dependent on anybody."

They will gain both the respect of those around them and the resources to care for themselves. They will gain power.

In an ideal world, being a Christian in the workplace would bring immediate respect and credibility. Unfortunately, the opposite is true in some communities. Many people become wary when believers use the word *Christian* to describe their life and work. On too many occasions, Christians have used their identity as leverage to justify a poor work ethic, shoddy workmanship, or failure to deliver on a promise. Paul says that the opposite should be true: Christians should be known as the most reliable people with whom to conduct business.

Paul comments on personal responsibility in another of his letters, the book of Colossians. There, the apostle gives advice to slaves and masters. While we can think of slavery only in terms of the horrendous terms of the North American slave trade of previous centuries, Paul wrote in a much different context. While still objectionable, the slavery of Paul's day was regulated by laws that required masters to treat slaves with much greater respect, and slaves were often given positions of great responsibility. With some highly notable exceptions, the situation then was analogous to employment in our day. We can read Paul's advice in Colossians 3:22–25 through the lens of the modern employer or employee.

> Slaves, obey your earthly masters in everything; and do it, not only when their eye is on you and to win their favor, but with sincerity of heart and reverence for the Lord. Whatever you do, work at it with all your heart, as working for the

Lord, not for men, since you know that you will receive an inheritance from the Lord as a reward. It is the Lord Christ you are serving. Anyone who does wrong will be repaid for his wrong, and there is no favoritism.

From Paul's advice to slaves and masters, we gather two important principles for the exercise of personal responsibility in the workplace.

The Everything Principle. First, Paul identifies what I call the everything principle: "Obey your earthly master *in everything*" (emphasis mine). This obligates us to be responsible in all areas of our work rather than taking responsibility only for selected things. I've discovered that some of my workplace responsibilities come naturally to me. Other responsibilities, equally important, don't come naturally. I have to be intentional about giving adequate effort to them. To insure that I faithfully fulfill these responsibilities, I often seek accountability from others. Conflict resolution is part of my job, but I'm a conflict avoider by nature. When presented with a conflict in which I have some responsibility for creating a resolution, I ask a coworker to hold me accountable to set the appointment or make the phone call that is necessary to address the problem. I want to fulfill *all* of my responsibilities, not just the comfortable ones. Accountability helps to me to push through my discomfort.

The Eye-Service Principle. The second dimension of workplace responsibility mentioned by Paul is what I call the eye-service principle. That means doing your job not only when the boss's "eye is on you," but all the time. Eye-service employees put on a good show and appear to be contributing whenever the boss is watching. But when the boss's attention is elsewhere, the quality and quantity of their work diminishes. Their service to their employer is superficial and insincere.

These two principles for workplace responsibility provide another occasion for self-assessment. Rate yourself on the following from 0 to 5 for each of the following statements.

_____ When something goes wrong at work, I take responsibility for my part in it rather than trying to shift blame.

_____ I fulfill all my responsibilities, not just the ones that come easily or comfortably.

_____ I work diligently whether or not the boss is around to notice.

_____ I seek accountability from coworkers that will reinforce my will to accomplish the responsibilities for which I have the least enthusiasm.

Respect for Authority

Paul's third advice for exercising power in the workplace is to have respect for authority. In Colossians 3:22–25, Paul speaks to employees about the importance of making their boss look good—but notice who he identifies as the true boss in the following phrases (emphasis mine).

- "[Work] with sincerity of heart and *reverence for the Lord*."
- "As *working for the Lord*, not for men."
- "Since you know that you will receive an *inheritance from the Lord as a reward*."
- "It is the *Lord Christ you are serving*."

According to these verses, all Christians—regardless of their position on the company's organizational chart—ultimately report to the same boss. No matter who may be our immediate supervisor, we all report to God.

I utilize the 360-degree performance review to gain insight on my job performance. This review includes feedback from all those with whom I work. I begin by distributing an evaluation form to our church's Local Board of Administration, to which I report. I distribute the same form to those who report directly for me. I then meet with each member of the board to share the compiled results of the evaluation as well as to discuss their particular evaluation of me. The 360-degree review process is a thorough one, but it is incomplete because it doesn't give me the entire picture. I like to lay the results of that review before the Lord and pray through each area, seeking to hear what my Ultimate Boss would say to me about each area. This exercise is a tangible reminder to me that I don't ultimately work for the church board, as much as I value their authority. I work for God and must submit to His authority.

And what about people who own their own business or at the top of their company's organizational chart? Paul has something to say to them as well: "Masters, provide your slaves with what is right and fair, because you know that you also have a *Master in heaven*. (Col. 4:1, emphasis mine). The words *I'm the boss* can be used only in a provisional sense. Each of us has a heavenly boss whose authority is eternal.

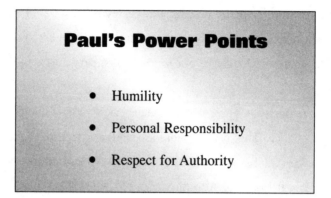

Paul's Power Points

- Humility
- Personal Responsibility
- Respect for Authority

What is your level of respect for authority in your work? Rate yourself from 0 to 5 in the following areas concerning your submission to God's authority so that you might be a person of influence in your workplace.

____ My primary focus is not on pleasing my immediate supervisor but on pleasing God.

____ I am more concerned with gaining an eternal reward than with my earthly salary and benefits.

____ Although I am "in charge" at work, I frequently remind myself that I am accountable to God for my use of the power entrusted to me.

When Christians are known for their integrity, for the quality of their work, and for relating to others in a way that empowers them to succeed, they please their Ultimate Boss. They also tend to become more powerful in their workplaces and to be given even greater opportunities to manage God's power. When we believe that we have a right to power, we are likely to be corrupted by it. When we humbly recognize that the authority we hold is a gift to be wisely used, we use power well.

For Further Thought

1. Have you occupied a seat of power or had a chance to observe someone who has? What did you discover about the effects of power on the one who holds it?

2. How might a Christian pray concerning his or her work and influence in the workplace?

3. The author takes the point of view that Christians should seek to maximize their use of power in the workplace. Do you agree that it is appropriate for believers to be power seekers?

4. What do you need to know in order to use power more effectively in your work? What disciplines can you adopt that will enable you to become a lifelong learner?

5. With whom do you need to build relationships in order to use power more effectively in your work?

6. What additional resources do you need in order to enhance your use of power at work? Where can you go to acquire those resources?

7. Why do you think Jesus connected greatness with servanthood in Matthew 20:26–28?

8. The author continually points to the fact that believers are primarily under the authority of God and should look to Him first for

both resources and approval. Do you find this concept to be empowering? Why or why not?

9. In what ways can an employee empower an employer?

10. What did you discover about your use of power by completing the self-assessments included in this chapter? What actions will you take to improve your stewardship of power as a result?

The Power to Influence

Arena of Power:	Church
Source of Power:	Integrity
Power Principle:	Power must be applied for the benefit of others.

I received this e-mail describing a series of power plays that threaten the health and future of a local church. It came from a disheartened pastor—I'll call him Nick—who is fearful for his own ministry as well the possibility that the power plays may undermine the progress his congregation has recently made. Nick, writes—

> I've been at the church for less than a year, and things have been going well—until now. I've made a few minor changes in the church's style of worship, but nothing drastic. In general, my ministry here has been well received. But there are a couple of people on the church board who are nothing short of antagonistic. One woman frequently throws jabs at me

over the most mundane things. Another fellow doesn't seem to have a positive bone in his body; he constantly points out the negative in everything, especially my job performance.

That's not the worst of it. Recently a couple in the church went to my denominational supervisor, telling him that I should be removed from the church because it's "falling apart." They named several people who were supposedly unhappy. Yet when my supervisor followed up with these people, they all said that wasn't the case.

The wife serves on an important committee in our church and exerts tremendous control over the congregation. I really think she should be removed from that committee because of her undermining actions, and my supervisor agrees. But our church board doesn't see it that way and believes we should talk with this couple to try to resolve the conflict. In the meantime, they have quit attending the church but haven't quit stirring things up. She is still officially a member of the committee.

Wayne, it feels like I'm losing control here. I was voted out of my last church because a small group of people banded together and created a great wave of problems. Now this . . . I'm just not sure what to do.

I would love to believe that this e-mail represents an isolated incident within the body of Christ, but more than twenty-five years in church leadership tell me otherwise. Local churches are frequently caught up in power plays, which leave in their wake the broken hearts of both pastors and parishioners. Many believers, however, are comfortable ignoring that reality. Their attitude toward church conflict is much like the philosophy I've seen stated on a bumper sticker: "Reality—a nice place to visit, but I wouldn't want to live there." In fact, power is used—and sometimes abused—in the church just as it is in the home, family, or workplace. We must take the use of power in this arena seriously.

Power may be applied in various forms. Elected officials have power by virtue of their position. Trusted employees have power by virtue of their knowledge or experience. In either case, an individual can choose either to use that power well or to abuse it. So it is the heart of the power-full person—not the specific means of power— that make the use of power either helpful or abusive.

The church is the arena in which the integrity of those using power comes most clearly into focus. Some of those who use power in the church, like Ananias and Sapphira, who gave the appearance of making a sacrificial gift while holding back something for themselves, do so with illegitimate motives. That sad incident from the book of Acts illustrates the principle that in the church, above all other places, power must be applied for the benefit of others.

The Reality of Power in the Church

Power is a fact of life. The use of power "is implicit in all human interaction—familial, sexual, occupational, national and international— either covertly or overtly."[1] Given the fact that the church is a place of intense human interaction, it should be no surprise that power comes into play there often. It is implicit in our relationships as brothers and sisters in Christ. Yet we often ignore the reality of power in the church. While a healthy distrust of power may be a good thing, the denial of its existence can only lead to the abuse of power. At a minimum, the result will be that churches fail to fulfill their God-given mission. At worst, ignorance of power in the church can provide a ripe setting for sin. It is vital that both pastors and laypeople understand the reality of power in the church and have a clear idea of how it can be abused.

Abuse of Inspiration

During my early teen years, our church was served by a wonderful pastor; I loved this man for his warmth, charisma, and approachability. He believed in me and affirmed some of my emerging talents, and his presence in my life was a tremendous blessing. Yet because my parents were always careful about exposing their children to conflicts at church, I was unaware that there were problems with this man's leadership—and his character.

One day the pastor's wife returned to her hometown in a different part of the country. Our congregation was told that there was some illness in the extended family and that she had gone to provide care. As the weeks went by, that reason her absence began to wear thin. Another was offered. Eventually it was revealed that the pastor and his wife were separated and that she planned to file for divorce. Rumors began to swirl about the long-term difficulties in their marriage and an inappropriate relationship between the pastor and a woman in our church.

Although it was over thirty-five years ago, I vividly remember the pastor's final Sunday at our church. He stood before the congregation to announce that he was leaving and would be starting another church nearby. He also stated that our dynamic music leader would be joining him in this new church. Then the pastor invited everyone to come join him on the next Sunday to be part of this fresh and exciting new venture.

I was stunned.

The next Sunday it was apparent that nearly half of our congregation had accepted this invitation to worship elsewhere. Friends I had seen at church for years were no longer there because their parents had decided to join the new church. Most of our youth group was gone, including its leaders. As a result, I was given my first leadership opportunity as president of the youth group. It was a job nobody else wanted in a group that practically no one attended.

I loved our pastor and the church. My sense of loss, anger, guilt, and sadness was nearly overwhelming as I realized that my church would never be the same and that I would likely never see the pastor again. Feeling those strong emotions during those formative years changed me just as our church was changed forever. It took many years to process and fully grieve that experience.

Because I was young and my parents exercised discretion, I have no idea what might have been happening behind the scenes. Perhaps the pastor was treated in ways that led him to feel justified in splitting the church. Maybe his contribution to the problems in his marriage and the accusation of an inappropriate relationship were greatly exaggerated; I don't know. Yet I do know this: he had been granted a position of spiritual power in the life of our church, and exercised that power for personal advantage. He abused his power in the area of inspiration. When he failed to question the source of his intended action, his use of power became self-generated and self-serving. As a result, he significantly weakened the church he had been called to strengthen.

The power of inspiration can be a wonderful gift to a church. It can raise the level of faith and confidence in a congregation. It can lead people to move beyond their comfort zones and act upon convictions that glorify God. In my own ministry, I have sought to harness that power in ways that keep me from abusing it. In annual one-on-one meetings with our governing board members, I ask whether they are detecting hobby-horse issues in my teaching. When I'm preparing to deliver a missional message, I run it by key leaders to be sure it resonates with them. I look for alignment between the inspiration I sense and the direction our church leaders have affirmed as healthy for the congregation. I always try to surround the use of inspiration with reflection in order to hear the whisper of God's Spirit regarding His involvement in inspiration power.

Abuse of Intelligence

Pastors are not the only ones whose power plays can damage a local church, and the abuse of power within a congregation is not limited to the area of inspiration. The power of information can be abused as well.

A couple of times a year I have the privilege of speaking at gatherings of pastors and their spouses. These retreats usually include a bit of free time between sessions, which provides the opportunity for some meaningful and revealing conversations. During one such break, I spoke with a pastor named Jack about his ministry setting, and he shared with me that he had recently assumed the leadership of the church after spending several years as pastor of another one. Almost immediately, the pain of his previous pastoral experience began to pour out.

Jack's previous congregation had a church boss—a powerful lay leader who was used to calling the shots at the church and having things go his way. This man was the vice-chairman of the church board, the highest position of formal power for a lay person in that congregation. The man's wife was the church secretary, and in that position was privy to a great deal of information about the workings of the church and the lives of the people in it. She readily shared that information with her husband. The combination of this couple's long experience within the church, his formal position of leadership, and her detailed knowledge of the congregation made this man a truly power-full person.

For several years prior to Jack's arrival, the church had been a revolving door, cycling pastors in and out every year or so. The cycle followed a predictable pattern: the church boss would be gracious to each pastor as he arrived; but as the pastor's influence began to grow, the powerful layperson would use position and knowledge to plant seeds of discontent. Soon the pastor's effectiveness would be undermined by a lack of support, and he would move on. Then the church boss would graciously receive the next pastor until his influence began to grow, and the cycle would continue.

Jack was determined to break that cycle. When the tide turned in his relationship with the church boss, Jack decided to resist the pressure to move on. He was aided by the fact that several other board members had become aware of the unhealthy pattern in their church and believed it was time for change. When the vice-chairman began a rumor, Jack would bring the "issue" to the church board and straighten out the story. As the power play continued to unfold, the vice-chairman's wife left her position as church secretary, which only made the man more determined to oppose Jack's leadership.

When the situation came to a head, the board members supported their pastor as he confronted the man. Being directly confronted was not something this church boss was used to, and he didn't like it. Dealing openly with conflict robbed him of power, which was based on the misuse of information. The man decided to leave the church, and he did not leave quietly. Several supporting members of the church left with him, at his invitation. Others in the church simply grew weary of the constant tension and chose to withdraw themselves from the church. When the dust had settled, fully half of the attendees had left.

The church had not been large to begin with, and at half strength it was struggling to survive. Budget reductions were necessary. Because the pastor's salary was the largest expense it was also the most tempting to eliminate, so the church board decided to reduce the pastor's salary and begin a bivocational arrangement. As a result, Jack was effectively forced to leave the church for financial reasons. Although Jack had sought to lead with integrity and finally did break the vice-chairman's stranglehold on church affairs, the man's abusive exercise of power, even in his absence, devastated both the church and this pastor's family.

The abuse of information flourishes in a church culture that is void of biblical communication—where there is gossip, slander, and innuendo. No wonder God considers things like grumbling a sin while we tend to justify it. Information power is positively expressed when we speak the truth in love, when our communication is focused on those who can be part of the solution, when it is used to serve and resource others.

Abuse of Influence

As a pastor, I realize that the line between the legitimate and illegitimate uses of power can be a blurry one. Even people who are rightly motivated can slip into the abusive use of their influence in the church. Several years ago I gathered with a group of pastors for a time of learning and encouragement. Because we had all known one another for some time, we were able to be transparent about tough leadership challenges and speak our minds. This was mostly a good thing, but there were times when it revealed how easy it is for leaders to adopt questionable, even sinful, power practices.

At one point, we commented on the courage required to make controversial decisions. The Bible is full of admonitions to "be strong and courageous." Personally, I am convinced the leaders God uses most effectively aren't necessarily smarter or more gifted than others but are more courageous. They are willing to act when others are paralyzed. They are willing to risk when others remain mired in their comfort zones. I shared those thoughts with the group.

As the discussion progressed, however, I realized how easily the concept of biblical courage can be perverted by power. Some pastors began to talk of a "body count"—meaning a number of attendees leaving the church—after implementing some decisions. I sensed that this body count was something like a badge of pride with some of the pastors. One bragged about how many people left when he initiated a change in the church's worship style. Others were motivated to top that story by relating their own experiences of "winning" conflicts. Attendees who had left the churches were labeled losers or troublemakers.

Eventually someone asked if a high body count was a sign of healthy change or a symptom of the abuse of power. The discussion got really lively at that point! It was a great question, and one I wished I'd asked.

Church leaders—clergy and lay—have tremendous influence over the lives of others. To use that influence wisely is a great challenge. Yet when that challenge is met, it can change the patterns within or the direction of a church. For that to happen, the power of influence must be used selflessly rather than selfishly. This power must be used strategically so that it moves people who are negative about the church to a position of neutrality and people who are neutral about the church to a place of positive contribution.

Abuse of Investment

The abuse of religious power is hardly new. Jesus directed his strongest anger at those who utilized their power in spiritually destructive ways. David Prior observes, "The dangers inherent in holding religious power are exposed in Matthew 23: there is little reason to suppose that these dangers have changed, let alone disappeared, in the last two thousand years."[2] The religious leaders in Jesus' day had what we would call high investment. They had significant resources at their command, and they had the will to commit themselves to action. In Matthew 23 Jesus accuses them of abusing power by—

- Imposing heavy burdens on their followers (23:3–4),
- Seeking to impress others rather than ministering to the deepest needs of people (23:5–6),
- Manifesting an exclusivist mentality that marginalized those who did not agree with them (23:16–22),
- Overemphasizing things of little value to the neglect of those that matter most (23:23–24),
- Covering up inner corruption while keeping up a good front externally (23:27–28).

Accounts in the other Gospels add to these accusations, saying that these power abusers were "lovers of money" (Luke 16:14) and plotters against those who threatened their power (Matt. 12:14; Mark 12:13). Church leaders have capital in the form of power. That capital can be invested to serve their own needs—often the maintenance of their own positions—or to serve others. Richard Foster notes,

In the church, power is to be used to inspire faith, not conformity. Bishops, pastors, elders, deacons and others have real power over people and should use it for life, not death. In matters that are essential to our spiritual growth, we want to do all we can to rouse people to action. But we must frankly admit that many things in our church life have little to do with righteousness, peace and joy in the Holy Spirit.[3]

Sources of Power within the Church

There are many ways to characterize the sources of power present in a church. Power-full church leaders may gain their power in any number of ways—from their elected positions, their family connections, their level of learning, and even their spiritual experience. I think it is helpful to think of these sources of power in three broad categories: institutional, individual, and informal. Awareness of the power residing in each and a commitment to good stewardship of all creates a healthy church.

Institutional Power

Institutional power is present in all organizations. It is built into the structures themselves. Local churches, districts, synods, classes, denominations, and even parachurch ministries all have built-in power grids. Sometimes those institutional power structures function well. Sometimes they do not, as David Pryor points out: "The power of the institutional church, both in its ecclesiastical structures and in its sluggish response to change, leaves most Christians in a confusion of screaming frustration and sad resignation."[4] Usually, it is not the institutions themselves but the poor stewardship of power within them that leads to the "screaming frustration." Sadly, this frustration affects not only those within the church but those whom it seeks to reach. They may be in Christ but turned off by the ineffectiveness of the church.

Many people only think of institutional power as negative, but it has several positive possibilities. Institutions have the power to convene groups or meetings that solve problems and create options. They have the power to nominate, appoint, or elect leaders who can be difference makers. Institutions can make heroes of people who reflect their vision and values, effectively telling their stories. A negative bias toward institutional power may cause us to miss its benefits.

Influenced by Age. Institutional power is affected by many variables. For example, churches with older members most often have a higher degree of institutional power than do churches with younger members. In fact, younger people often see little value in the institution itself, preferring to think of the church only in terms of relationships. Younger people sometimes take great pains to model newly formed congregations in reaction to the institutional power they've encountered in the past.

The local church I serve belongs to a denomination that includes a level of organization called the *district.* Our district comprises fifty congregations in western Michigan. This district has long had the intention to be aggressive in planting new congregations and in recent years has translated that intention into action. By doing so, the district has exercised institutional power. Yet every new church that has been planted has lessened the institutional power of our district. Why? Because new churches, led by entrepreneurial pastors, are usually very effective in reaching unchurched people and leading them to Christ. Those newer congregations, filled with people who were recently unchurched and led by entrepreneurial pastors, are unlikely to have much concern for the institutions of the district or denomination. So as the percentage of new churches in our district increases, it is inevitable that the district will have less institutional power. Is that a negative thing? Not necessarily. Yet I am convinced that it is a subtle yet potent reality that keeps many institutional leaders from aggressively planting new local churches.

Influenced by Size. Church size is another factor that influences institutional power. Years ago Lyle Schaller developed a helpful typology for understanding congregations.[5] He rightly observed that as churches grow they not only get bigger but also change fundamentally. The result is that institutional power is relocated—and that relocation can prompt the dislocation of people who have been a part of the church. Some have hypothesized that every time a church doubles in size, it outgrows half of its leadership. Here is an overview of Schaller's typology along with my observations about the use of power in churches.

1. The Fellowship Church. Churches with fewer than thirty-five attendees, Schaller compares to a cat. No one ever owns a cat—they're much too independent for that. And while the demise of a tiny congregation may be often predicted, it seldom occurs. As everyone knows, a cat has nine lives. In these congregations, power rests with the people, not with the pastor (they've endured many) or the denomination (they refuse to sit on command). There are approximately one hundred thousand congregations of this size in North America.

2. The Small Church. Churches having from thirty-five to one hundred in attendance, Schaller compares to a collie. Like collies, these congregations want to love and be loved, and they are very responsive to their leaders. Power rests with the congregation;

but in churches of this size, that power is concentrated in lay or pastoral leaders. One third of the churches in North America are small churches.

3. The Mid-Sized Church. Churches having from 100 to 175 in attendance, Schaller compares to a garden. A gardener's work is never done, so the leaders of these congregations must both love gardening and have added skill in planning. Power rests with key leaders in these congregations, increasingly with the pastor and with those who have greater planning and leadership skills.

4. The Awkward Size Church. Churches having from 175 to 225 in attendance, Schaller compares to a house. These churches are more work than one minister can handle, but they generally feel that they can't afford more staff. Like a house, these churches include specialized rooms representing special interest groups. Churches of this size encounter the notorious "200 barrier." To move beyond it, there must be a change in how the pastor relates to the congregation and how the congregation members relate to one another. In churches of this size, power resets increasingly with the pastor as well as those who care for some of the rooms in the house (that is, ministry leaders). This is usually the largest-sized church that can be controlled by the members of one extended family.

5. The Large Church. Churches having from 225 to 450 in attendance, Schaller compares to a mansion. To navigate a mansion, visitors need directional signs and assistance from staff specialists. A mansion may include a few cats, maybe a collie or two, and at least one garden. Power in a large church rests with the pastor, a staff of specialists, key lay leaders, and perhaps certain power blocks within the congregation.

6. The Huge Church. Churches having from 450 to 700 in attendance, Schaller compares to a ranch. The pastor is a rancher who must see the big picture over a long period of time. Because the scope of the work is vast, the pastor must avoid a do-it-yourself approach. He or she cannot be a veterinarian, gardener, or housekeeper. Power rests with pastor, pastoral staff, and key lay leaders. Often, conflict occurs as responsibilities that were once filled by laypersons are turned over to "professionals."

7. The Mini-Denomination Church. Churches having over 700 in attendance, Schaller compares to a nation. The president of a nation is vulnerable to criticism and, therefore, works closely with representative groups and fulfills a role that may not be fully understood by the majority of people. Because congregations of this size can survive without the support of a denomination, there may be tension between the church and its denomination. Power rests with the pastor and key staff specialists. While smaller churches function as participatory democracies, churches of this size may be either representative democracies or benign dictatorships.

Reflecting on the dynamics of life within congregations of various sizes, it is easy to see how the application of power is affected by church size. In smaller churches, power is most often concentrated in a lay person or a prominent family or families. In larger churches, power is usually concentrated in the pastor and the pastor's team of professional or lay leaders.

Does Schaller's typology fit your congregation? Where does the institutional power rest in your church?

Individual Power

Individual power in the context of the church is the power that is present in a person, not an organization. That person may be a pastor, a board member, a lay leader, a denominational executive, or a leader within an educational or parachurch organization. Individuals are accountable to God and to others for their stewardship of power.

We often think of the poor stewardship of power in terms of individuals who abuse power by exercising it inappropriately or too frequently. The failure to exercise God-given power when necessary is equally poor stewardship. We can picture the stewardship of individual power as a continuum.

Passive   Powered Up

Powered Up versus Passive. At one time in my ministry, I was interacting with two pastoral colleagues whose use of power might be represented on opposite ends of the continuum. One colleague could easily have been nicknamed Napoleon—not because of his stature but because he led his church like a general. Those who expressed opinions that diverged from his were considered insubordinate. I recall coming away from our meetings together feeling that I wasn't a leader at all—his commanding presence was intimidating to me and to others. Over time, however, his tendency to power up on anyone who didn't immediately see things his way created weakness in his church and leadership team. If wasn't long before these vulnerabilities undermined his credibility and destroyed his opportunity to lead the church in the future. He left the church without ever coming to grips with the power dynamics that contributed to his downfall.

During the same time period, I was also meeting with another colleague whose leadership style was very passive. He related stories of board members who were encouraging him to exercise stronger leadership and provide a sense of direction to the church. He disclosed that one board member was literally begging him to step into the leadership vacuum his passivity was creating. He did not, and soon the leadership vacuum was filled by a layperson whose vision for the church severely limited its potential for the future. While this pastor stayed on for years—and was loved by many of the church members—the church soon reached a plateau and then slowly declined under his power shortage.

Neither powering up nor being passive is good stewardship of power. One approach resorts to strong-arm tactics, the other is too limp-wristed to lead. Wise stewards recognize the fact that power has been entrusted to them and humbly invest that power to turn intention into action.

Power Questions. The use of individual power involves asking the *what* question. Just as God asked Moses, "What is that in your hand?" (Exod. 4:2), so each leader must discern what power God has placed under his or her management.

The use of individual power also involves asking the *when* question: is this God's timing for the intended action? I've heard many

pastors wonder if the time was right to exercise their influence by investing their credibility in making a change they perceived would benefit the
church they served. Lay leaders often struggle with this same question of
timing. If I have a dream for the direction that a ministry, program, or
church should take in the future, how will I know *when* to make changes?

Be cautious of making generalizations about when to exercise
power. Some pastors believe they should never make a significant
change in the first year of their ministry. While it is generally true that
power tends to increase with tenure, waiting a year in some situations
will produce too little change too late. Other leaders see their selec-
tion or election as a mandate for change. They make necessary
changes too soon, causing people to feel that they are being force-fed
and force-led. Prayerful discernment is the only way to sense God's
timing in the stewardship of power.

The application of individual power also involves asking the
where question: in what area am I able to exercise power? Individuals
are powerful in different ways in different settings. Some have the
power to innovate—their best contribution comes in the creation of
vision and ideas. Others have power to influence—they have a
tremendous capacity to sell the vision and direction to others. Still
others have the power to implement—they can create the structures
and processes that provide the path for vision to become reality.

Years ago I served on a membership study committee for my
denomination. I had just completed my doctoral project on the subject
of membership and, in the process, had come to some firm convictions
that were dramatically different from the church's current membership

practices. Other members of the committee and some of the decision makers in my denomination seemed to appreciate the research and creativity of the recommendations I brought to the committee. However, those recommendations didn't get very far. On that committee, I had a lot of innovation power but little influence power, and without the support of key influencers, my proposals went nowhere.

During that same time, I was serving as chairman of the board in the local church that I serve. I noticed that when proposals were presented to the board, my support, or the absence of it, was taken very seriously by other board members. I also was frequently responsible for leading the staff in implementing any proposals that were adopted. I wasn't the most innovative member of the board, but I had considerable power for influencing the acceptance of proposals and implementing them so they became reality.

As an individual, what power has God entrusted to you in your local church? When are you to exercise that power? Where is that power most clearly needed, and in what ways can you contribute to turn intention into action?

Informal Power

Informal power is not evident on organizational charts and cannot be definitely located in an individual leader, but it is nonetheless real. Informal power is evident in the longtime church member who, with the nod of his or her head, determines the outcome of a vote. It is seen in the major contributor whose facial expression is read by everyone concerned about the financial stability of the church.

Framing. One expression of informal power relates to the framing of a discussion—the creation of a certain perception about a situation. Perception, whether right or wrong, creates the reality to which people hold. Framing is the process by which people attempt to impose their preferred vision of reality on situations, and it happens in four ways:

- Explicitly—By aggressively arguing for a particular characterization of a specific situation or event.
- Implicitly—By behaving as if a situation were a certain way, perhaps by acting alarmed in relation to someone else's characterization of the facts.
- Indirectly—By supporting someone who is arguing or acting in a way that favors one interpretation rather than another.
- Politically—By trading favors or becoming so important or intimidating to certain others that these intimidated individuals figure out ways to structure situations to support and appease opinion makers without their ever having to voice an explicit opinion.[6]

Framing is an often-used power tool in the church. During the denominational membership study process I referred to earlier, one group would frame its viewpoint as biblical and opposing views as legalistic. Another group would frame its viewpoint as convictional and other viewpoints as liberal. I've also seen framing used during a board meeting discussing a potential building program. In such situations, one group typically frames its conservative approach as "wisdom" while the other sees its more aggressive approach as "exercising faith."

Labeling. On one occasion I met with two wonderful couples whose hearts were breaking over certain events that had taken place at the church they had previously attended. They had let me know that they believed there were significant problems with the pastoral leadership in that church. They'd asked for the meeting because they wanted to share their story. I admit that I went to the meeting with my guard up; I've learned that when people have problems with one pastor, they are likely to have similar problems with the next one.

As the conversation progressed, I could see that they were not vindictive or bitter, but they were deeply hurt. They had been part of a large church that had parented a daughter congregation. The large church was known in our community for its high level of integrity, but also for being suspicious of anyone who questioned authority in any way. These couples had felt led to be part of the core group of this new church plant. They invested heavily of their time, talents, and treasures in helping to start the new congregation. As anyone who has been part of a church plant knows, the early days are often the most demanding. Happily, this core group slowly developed into a fledgling church.

As the new church developed, though, the pastor became less collegial and more authoritative in his approach. Significant decisions were often made without discussion among the leadership team, and any questioning or constructive evaluation was labeled as divisive. The pastor used his positional power to *frame* anyone who disagreed with him or even asked clarifying questions.

As the pastor increasingly elevated himself above the new congregation and used "fresh revelations from God" as a means of marginalizing other people in the decision making process, these couples decided to approach the pastor of the parent church to seek counsel. That pastor declined to meet with them because he was concerned that by doing so he would embolden and empower "the opposition." By the power of framing, these couples went from being key supporting members to being "the opposition." They were not negative consumers at the church; they simply had honest questions that deserved honest answers.

I realize that one meeting does not provide enough opportunity to discern a person's true intentions or character. Yet as these couples joined our church and began to serve in various ministries, they turned out to be wonderful servant-leaders. One of the four eventually joined our staff. Yes, they still ask good questions that force us to clarify our ministry goals and search our motives. But that has made our church stronger, not weaker.

Framing in the form of labeling is one of the most common abuses of power. All organizations are capable of it. People may be identified as "troublemakers" or it may be said that they are "not team players." Labeling has even greater power in churches, where it tends to be spiritualized. Those who disagree with authority may be labeled as "divisive," "insubordinate," or even "carnal."

Framing and labeling are two examples of the use of informal power. Informal power is often hard to discern because of its subtlety. This subtlety is the very thing that increases the impact of informal power—the less obvious it is, the more powerful it becomes.

Power Shifts

Describing the realms of power in three neat categories may create the misimpression that they are readily identified and fairly static. In most local churches, all three forms of power are simultaneously at work and are constantly shifting. In the history of nearly every local church, there are *tipping points* when the sources of power exercised within the church dramatically and suddenly change. Just as the shift of tectonic plates beneath the earth's surface create earthquakes and tsunamis, so these power shifts within a church can have a tremendous effect—for better or for worse—on the future well-being of the congregation and those within it. These are the times when proper stewardship of power is most needed.

These tipping points, or power shifts, will occur when the existing power brokers or power blocks feel they are losing control to emerging power brokers or blocks. When that happens, what would otherwise be considered small changes suddenly appear to be a major changes that represents a totally new direction for the church. Apparently overnight, new members who have been welcomed with open arms become a large enough group that their influence rivals that of the long-term stakeholders in the congregation.

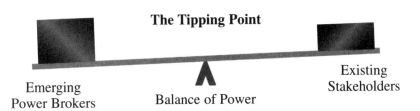

The Tipping Point

Emerging
Power Brokers

Balance of Power

Existing
Stakeholders

Carl George speaks to pastors about these power shifts, but his encouragement applies to lay leaders as well: "Every organization includes a huge contingent of people called stakeholders—those with an investment in what you are doing. They care very deeply that in your enthusiastic pursuit of the organization's future you do not forget the *powerful* contingent who helped create the past"[7] (emphasis mine).

It is important that leaders, as wise stewards of power, be proactive in addressing any polarization that develops between long-term stakeholders and newcomers. When that polarization shows itself, the leader's temptation will be to ally him- or herself with the group that seems most powerful, thus either preserving control for the old guard or helping the newcomers to forge a new direction. That is a mistake. As newcomers gain power, stakeholders may feel neglected and retaliate by using their power to hurt the pastor. Newcomers who do not feel that they are gaining their rightful place at the table may come to feel frustrated and lash out in similar ways. This kind of strained relationship leads to forced terminations or church splits. Inevitably, leaders in any local church must come to realize that they do not preside over one unified congregation but over various groups within the whole. Leaders must, therefore, seek to determine what each group needs.

When the balance of power reaches a tipping point, those who hold power must return to the questions of inspiration, intelligence, influence, and investment. They must make certain that their exercise of power is neither self-generated nor self-serving, and then marshal their influence and resources to unite the church around the action that best meets the needs of *the whole*.

Resources of Power

People are powerful in different ways because they draw their power from different resources. I remember gathering with a group of pastors of large churches, each of whom was powerful within his or her own congregation. Ironically, this group of high-powered pastors had trouble making the simplest of decisions regarding their future meetings. I watched as several of them attempted to influence the direction of the group. Some used words, some used the power of personal relationships, others drew power from their seniority in the group, and still others attempted to sway the group by presenting a detailed plan. It was clear that each of them understood the power tools that worked best for them. They were skilled in drawing upon those resources.

Resources

Every church—and every leader—has resources available to it. Good stewardship of power involves appropriately using those resources—and not abusing them. The ultimate resource for every congregation is found in its connection to God's power (see chapter

1). Jesus himself promised, "I will build my church, and the gates of hell will not prevail against it" (Matt. 16:18 KJV). In addition to that ultimate resource, there are others that a wise steward of power will cultivate. This partial list of power resources is a good beginning for any church member or leader.

Position. Power may be drawn from the *position* held by the leader. For instance, according to the constitution of the church that I serve, the senior pastor serves as the chairperson of the church board. Holding that position allows me to place certain items on the board's agenda— and to keep others off the agenda. If I use that power to highlight priorities that are in keeping with God's will for our church, that positional power benefits us all. However, if I were to use that power to quash healthy debate or discussion, it would weaken the leadership team.

Reward. A second power resource is reward. This is the power to offer incentives such as pay, promotion, or recognition. Institutionally, this power may be exercised by a committee that establishes salaries for staff members or by a denominational executive who can award loyal pastors greater opportunities for service. Individually, the power of reward may be exercised by a wealthy person who "rewards" the church with generous donations when the church does what he or she wants. Every pastor knows what a blessing it is to have generous givers, and it is a double blessing when they are able to give substantial amounts. That blessing can easily become a curse, however, when it is given conditionally.

Jim is a long-term member of his church and has served on the board for several years. A tithe of his weekly income amounts to approximately two hundred dollars per week—a welcome donation for the mid-sized church that he attends. But Jim uses the power of reward to manipulate the board's decisions. When the board chooses to adopt the projects that Jim favors, he tithes consistently. But when those projects are not adopted or are not implemented as Jim wishes, he withholds his tithe. Jim also has a number of "concerns" about the church. When the pastor fails to address those concerns to Jim's liking, he expresses his disapproval with his wallet.

In some cases, manipulative givers are quiet about their actions, but not Jim. He has made statements to the board like these:

- "If you don't continue to support this project, I want my money back!"
- "You'll never see another penny from me."
- "This church couldn't survive one week without my check."

Jim has the power to reward the church with his giving, but, unfortunately, he exercises that power in negative ways.

Coercion. A third power resource is *coercion.* This is the power to punish, remove, or induce compliance. It is based on intimidation or fear. Coercion may be applied by a financial contributor like Jim, or it may be used by a pastor who threatens a parishioner with pseudo-spiritual claims or an allegedly prophetic voice. Coercion may also be applied through the undue use of emotion.

Coercion is more often exercised in its potential rather than its actual form. When I was a child, my parents used the often-heard threat that begins "If I have to stop this car . . ." I don't remember if they ever did stop the car. They probably didn't have to; the threat alone was enough to cause me to reconsider my behavior. In fact, the threat of action is often more effective than the action itself. In churches, decisions are often made based on a feared result, not a proven reality. Statements such as "If we adopt this direction, half the congregation will leave" are often enough to prevent churches from making changes, even good ones.

Can coercion ever be a good thing? While it is the power of last resort, coercion can be necessary and beneficial to a church when properly applied. Pastors who are failing to fulfill their responsibilities may need their superiors to coerce them into facing reality and taking responsibility. Members who are engaged in sinful behavior can benefit from the exercise of church discipline, which often begins in a coercive manner but should ultimately be redemptive. Members who are disruptive or divisive can be removed from membership roles until they change their behavior. Coercion must be used cautiously, perhaps more so than other forms of power, but it can be beneficial.

Charisma. A fourth power resource is *charisma,* which in this case means the power accorded to a leader based on that leader's personal traits. This power is given if the group members like you, identify with you, or like what you stand for. As with most power resources, it can be used positively or negatively. This power can be used by a leader to motivate others to pursue what is best for all, or a leader may use his or her charisma to manipulate others for selfish ends.

175

A prominent faith healer held a service in our city, filling a local arena to capacity. A member of our church heads the company that provides security to the arena and had a behind-the-scenes view of the operation. While those in attendance were wowed by the music and message, this security chief watched as some people were turned away from seeking healing, witnessed the careful placement of certain individuals in the most prominent seats, and saw the buckets of money that were received after a carefully orchestrated and emotion-laden financial appeal. Sadly, that inside look at the use of the power of charisma at that event caused this man to doubt his recently found faith in Christ.

Expertise. A fifth power resource is *expertise*, which is drawn from a leader's knowledge and skill. Expertise generates respect, which is in turn used to influence others. In most congregations, the pastor is viewed as an expert on Scripture. This status as expert can be used to guide a congregation into truth and to refute error, or it can be used to misapply Scripture in an attempt to influence the direction of the church.

Information. Related to expertise is the power of *information.* The person holding information knows what is going on or has access to information that is perceived as valuable by others. It benefits any leader who is considering implementing a change to conduct some research on other churches who have already implemented a similar changes or to read books that describe the intricacies of the new approach. By doing "homework," the leader increases his or her expertise and becomes more influential in discussing the proposed change with others.

Connection. The resource of *connection* is also a source of power for church leaders. This power is drawn from the leader's connections with influential or important persons inside or outside the congregation. God uses mentors and other mature people to help leaders accomplish their goals. The power of connection inappropriately used results in namedropping, misquoting, or misrepresenting relationships with influential people.

Empowering

At the heart of the wise stewardship of the resources of power is the desire to empower others. Generally, power-full people face the temptation to use their power for personal gain. They must make the shift from *me-powering* to *empowering* others. The transposition of those first two letters makes a huge difference in the application of power resources, as Christian Schwartz points out.

> Leaders of growing churches concentrate on empowering other Christians for ministry. They do not use lay workers as "helpers" in attaining their own goals and fulfilling their own visions. Rather, they invert the pyramid of authority so that the leader assists Christians to attain the spiritual potential God has for them.[8]

Me Power ⟶ *Em*power

In other words, leaders who are wise stewards of power will not only manage well the power God has entrusted to them but also will help others to manage the power God has entrusted to them. I recognized this principle when writing the book *Ministry Momentum*.[9] I had researched the leadership strategies employed by the Old Testament leader Joshua as he led the people of God into the Promised Land. I discovered that the movement began with Joshua, to whom God had entrusted the vision for entering the Promised Land. Next to Joshua in their ability to exercise power were the officers of the army, who directed the military power. After them came the priests, who were the stewards of spiritual power in Israel. They were followed by leaders from each tribe, who exercised influence over their family-based groups. Last of all came the people. I observed that Joshua masterfully aligned diverse resources of power—military, spiritual, and tribal—to accomplish the goal. By using his power resources well, Joshua empowered a nation.

Leaders in local churches must do the same if they are to turn intention into action. As Warren Bennis and Burt Nanus point out, "Vision is the commodity of leaders, and power is their currency."[10] In order to successfully exercise power, we must pool our currency with that of others, then spend it wisely for God's glory.

For Further Thought

1. Why do you think many people ignore the power plays that happen within a local church?

2. Have you seen any of the abuses of power exhibited by the religious leaders of Jesus' day in religious leaders today?

3. Identify your church in Schaller's typology of church sizes. Where does the institutional power rest in your congregation?

4. Have you seen church leaders (pastoral or lay) who either powered up or remained passive when dealing with conflicts? What was the result of each power style?

5. What individual power has God entrusted to you within your local church? When and how have you exercised that power in the past? Where is that power most clearly needed at present?

6. Has your church ever experienced a tipping point when power shifted from one location to another within the congregation? What was the effect of that shift upon the church? Upon you personally?

7. Which of the power resources listed in this chapter have you seen used in a local church? Were those uses positive or negative?

8. The author states that all leaders must move from *me power* to *empower* in order to be good stewards of power. What might move a leader to make that shift?

Afterword

We all have power. Every one of us has the God-given ability to turn intention into action. Some of us have been entrusted with a greater or lesser share of power, but we are all power-full people in some degree. If we are to be good stewards of power, we must make the decision to use our power to serve God and others. Jesus' instruction to His disciples that they were not to "lord it over others" should ring often in the ears of today's believers as they live out their roles as spouses, parents, employees or employers, and church members or leaders. Jesus wanted them, and wants us, to understand the difference between the use of power that keeps others subservient to or dependent upon us and the use of power that sets them free. When our power is aligned with God's power, it prevails.

The proper stewardship of power begins within us. It involves the redeeming of our fallen nature as part of the human community. The power plays most difficult to manage can be the ones found inside the human heart.

What causes fights and quarrels among you? Don't they come from your desires that battle within you? You desire but do not have, so you kill. You covet but you cannot get what you want, so you quarrel and fight. You do not have because you do not ask God. When you ask, you do not receive, because you ask with wrong motives, that you may spend what you get on your pleasures (James 4:1–3).

What are our motives as we relate to God, our families, our coworkers, and fellow church members? Is our power self-generated and self-serving, or do we use power to serve God and others?

The exciting good news is that we *can* do this. Empowered by the Holy Spirit, we lay aside the destructive power tools and power plays that all too often characterize our interactions with family members, coworkers, and fellow believers. We can become transformed people who have a transforming effect upon the world around us.

Someday the power plays of earth will be replaced by the perfect use of power in heaven. All of the misuses and abuses of power so painfully prevalent here will then be banished under the triumphant dominion of the Lord himself. There, we will be gathered into a heavenly city, where God is on the throne and "his servants will serve him," and, as His servants, "they will reign forever and ever" (Rev. 22:3, 5). We will both serve and reign.

The familiar maxim is both biblical and reliable: "Serve faithfully here, rule perfectly there."[1] In anticipation of that glorious day, let us set aside all power games and manipulation so that we may live with strength and integrity. Let us use the power that God has entrusted us wisely, diligently, and well.

Notes

Introduction

1. Richard Swenson, *Restoring Margin to Overloaded Lives* (Colorado Springs, Colo.: NavPress, 1999), 7.

Chapter One

1. Robert Clinton, *The Making of a Leader* (Colorado Springs, Colo.: NavPress, 1988), 103.

2. Ibid, 102.

3. Paul Chilcote, *Praying in the Wesleyan Spirit*, (Nashville, Tenn.: Upper Room Books, 2001), 123–124.

4. An interview with Larry Crabb entitled "American Idols" in Leadership Journal, Summer 2004, p. 26.

5. John Maxwell, Willow Creek Association Leadership Summit, August 2005.

Chapter Two

1. Richard Foster, *Money, Sex, and Power* (San Francisco, Calif.: Harper and Row, 1985), 175.

2. Ibid.

3. Willard Harley, *His Needs, Her Needs* Grand Rapids, Mich.: Fleming H. Revell Company, 2001).

4. Olivia Mellan, *Money Harmony: Resolving Money Conflicts in Your Life and Relationships* (New York, N.Y.: Walker Publishing Company, 1994), 127.

5. Foster, *Money, Sex, and Power*, 207–208.

6. Ibid., 206.

7. Ibid., 201–202.

8. Sara Song, "What Pets Bring to the Party," *Time*, January 17, 2005, 38.

9. Anne and Ray Ortlund, *You Don't Have to Quit* (Nashville, Tenn.: Thomas Nelson Publishers, 1986), 20.

10. Ibid., 50.

11. Lewis Smedes, *Forgive and Forget: Healing the Hurts We Don't Deserve* (San Francisco, Calif.: Harper and Row, 1984), 185.

Chapter Three

1. Peter Scazzero with Warren Bird, *The Emotionally Healthy Church: A Strategy for Discipleship That Actually Changes Lives* (Grand Rapids, Mich.: Zondervan Publishing House, 2003). See Chapter 6, "Prnciple 2: Break the Power of the Past."

2. Marcus Buckingham and Donald O. Clifton, *Now, Discover Your Strengths* (New York, N.Y.: Free Press, 2001). Albert L. Winseman, Donald O. Clifton, Curt Liesveld, *Living Your Strengths: Discover Your God-Given Talents and Inspire Your Community* (New York, N.Y.: Gallup Press, 2004).

3. Lewis Smedes, *Forgive and Forget: Healing the Hurts We Don't Deserve*, (San Francisco, Calif.: Harper and Row, 1984), 176–177.

4. Ibid., 185.

5. Jen Abbas, *Generation Ex: Adult Children of Divorce and the Healing of Our Pain* (Colorado Springs, Colo.: Waterbrook Press, 2004), 27.

6. Willard F. Harley Jr., *His Needs, Her Needs for Parents: Keeping Romance Alive* (Grand Rapids, Mich.: Fleming H. Revell Company, 2003), 12.

7. David Prior, *Jesus & Power* (Wheaton, Ill.: Victor Books, 1979), 107.

8. Lawrence Kohlberg, *The Philosophy of Moral Development* (San Francisco, Calif.: Harper and Row, 1981), 409–412.

9. Ted Ward, *Values Begin at Home* (Wheaton, Ill.: Victor Books, 1979), 50.

Chapter Four

1. Warren G. Bennis and Burt Nanus, *Leaders: Strategies for Taking Charge* (New York, N.Y.: Harper and Row, 1985), 15.

2. Rosabeth Moss Kanter, *The Change Masters: Innovation and Entrepreneurship in the American Corporation* (New York, N.Y.: Simon and Schuster, 1983), 216.

3. Richard Foster, *Money, Sex, and Power*, (San Francisco, Calif.: Harper and Row, 1985), 211.

4. Kanter, *Change Masters,* 18.

5. Foster, *Money Sex, and Power,* 211.

6. Jim Colins, *Good to Great* (New York: HarperCollins Publishers, 2001), 17–40.

Chapter Five

1. Warren G. Bennis and Burt Nanus, *Leaders: Strategies for Taking Charge* (New York, N.Y.: Harper and Row, 1985), 15.

2. David Prior *Jesus and Power* (Downers Grove, Ill.: InterVarsity Press, 1988),126–127.

3. Richard Foster, *Money, Sex, and Power* (San Francisco, Calif.: Harper and Row, 1985), 209.

4. Prior, *Jesus and Power,* 11–12.

5. Lyle Schaller, *Looking in the Mirror* (Nashville, Tenn.: Abingdon Press, 1984), 14–37.

6. *Advances in Organization Development Vol. 1,* ed. Fred Massarik (Westport, Conn.: Ablex Publishing, 1990), 58.

7. Carl George, *How to Break Growth Barriers*(Grand Rapids, Mich.: Baker Book House, 1993), 109.

8. Christian A. Schwartz, *Natural Church Development* (Carol Stream, Ill.: Church Smart Resources, 1996), 22.

9. Wayne Schmidt, *Ministry Momentum* (Indianapolis, Ind.: Wesleyan Publishing House, 1996, 2004).

10. Warren G. Bennis and Burt Nanus, *Leaders: Strategies for Taking Charge* (New York, N.Y.: Harper and Row, 1985), 17.

Afterword

1. Bruce Wilkinson, *A Life God Rewards: Why Everything You Do Today Matters Forever* (Sisters, Ore.: Multnomah Publishers, 2002), 74.

Other Books
By Wayne Schmidt

Lead On

*Why Churches Stall and How
Leaders Get Them Going*

Paperback   192 pages
0-89827-261-0

Ministry
Momentum

*How to Get It, Keep It,
and Use It in Your Church*

Paperback   160 pages
0-89827-280-7

wesleyan
publishing
house

*igniting a passion for
God in all of life!*

www.wesleyan.org/wph